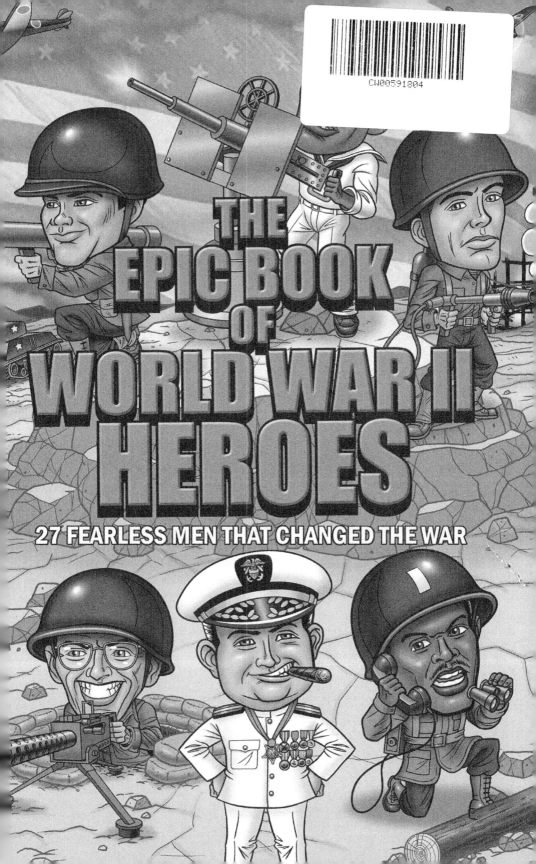

THE EPIC BOOK OF WORLD WAR II HEROES

27 FEARLESS MEN THAT CHANGED THE WAR

TABLE OF CONTENTS

INTRODUCTION

As of 2020, there are roughly 325,574 U.S. WWII veterans still living, of the sixteen million who participated in the war.

Each day that number is shrinking until none will be left to tell their stories.

The triumphs, losses, sacrifices, and unspeakable experiences that the greatest generation had burdened on their shoulders so that we who have come after them could inherit their priceless gift.

I wanted to collect some of their stories here to honor them and the incredible feats they accomplished, especially for those whom it cost them their very lives. I will warn you now that my writing style is very informal. It can come across as disrespectful especially when referring to the enemies the Allied forces fought during WW2. I know nothing but respect for the young men on all sides. They simply did what their country and leaders asked them to do.

Lives were lost on all sides. Families lost sons, husbands, brothers, uncles, and fathers. This fact is not lost on me though my writing may paint a different picture. As a fourth-generation military member, I know firsthand that something as ugly and chaotic as war can cut humanity to its core and just how powerful humor can be to cope.

As for the heroes captured here, I wanted to do more than simply rehash what is described on a medal citation. I wanted to bring their stories to life. It took digging into interviews, after action reports, books, newspaper articles, and first, second, and third hand accounts to pull all this information together. And yet, I am not truly satisfied with what I've uncovered knowing it will all pale in comparison to the real experiences that these incredible men encountered during the war to answer their nation's call.

The shifting sands of time has its way of distorting the facts of what really happened during the Second World War. Though I've been diligent with my research, the details of the accounts of these heroes are not without some error. However, I do not believe the potential minor errors, if any, take away from the heroic accomplishments. One thing is for sure, the stories captured here barely scratch the surface of all the heroes of that era.

This is only the beginning. For war history buffs, some of these names and their stories will be familiar. For the general audience, most of these individuals you will have never heard of along with their incredible stories. I hope you are inspired by their bravery and courage, their relentless pursuits and effort, and their enduring love for their country and the men they serve.

BEFORE YOU BEGIN

Hey reader, as a thank you for grabbing a copy of the book, I wanted to offer you a bonus book.

I've collected some whacky WW2 stories you will not believe are true.

Even as I was digging this up, I didn't believe some of them either, but the research checks out.

I wrote this book for my WW2 buffs who just can't get enough about the second world war.

To grab your free copy, scan the QR code below.

I can't wait to hear what you think!

CHAPTER 1

PEARL HARBOR HEROES

"Pearl Harbor caused our Nation to wholeheartedly commit to winning World War II, changing the course of our Nation's history and the world's future."
~ Joe Baca

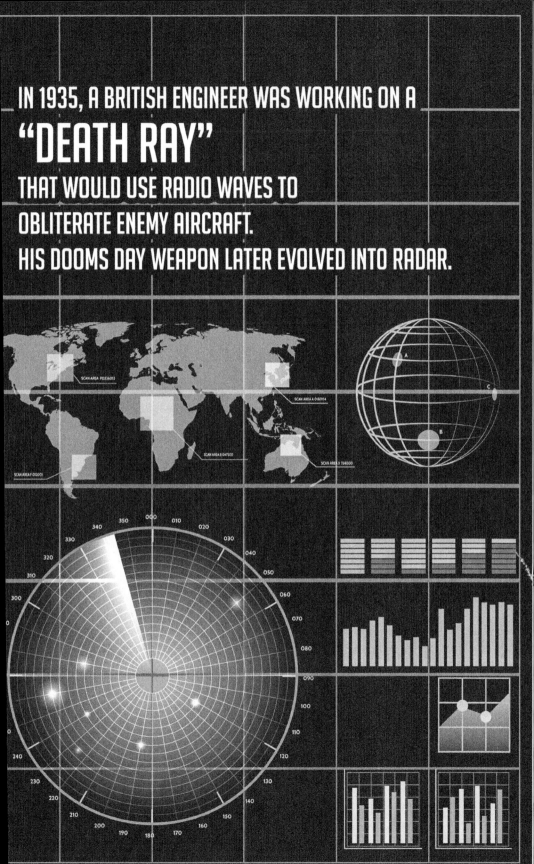

IN 1935, A BRITISH ENGINEER WAS WORKING ON A
"DEATH RAY"
THAT WOULD USE RADIO WAVES TO
OBLITERATE ENEMY AIRCRAFT.
HIS DOOMS DAY WEAPON LATER EVOLVED INTO RADAR.

DORIS "DORIE" MILLER

On December 7, 1941, what should have been an ordinary day at Pearl Harbor for the crew aboard the anchored USS West Virginia became a day the world would never forget.

Up at 6 a.m., Cook Third Class Doris "Dorie" Miller, a 22-year-old African American, had finished serving breakfast to the crew and was in the middle of collecting laundry, one of the very few jobs available to African Americans at the time.

At 7:57 a.m., a torpedo struck his ship bringing him straight to his knees. The alarm started blaring throughout the ship notifying the entire crew to head to their battle stations. This was not a drill nor an ordinary day. The USS West Virginia was under attack and the laundry would have to wait.

Within minutes, the ship was in flames as the Japanese attack continued. Miller headed straight to his battle station, a gun battery magazine amidship, ready to take names and help turn some Japanese pilots into swiss cheese. His job was to pass ammunition from within the magazine up to the gunners. Unfortunately, Miller found his battle station flooded from a torpedo which had destroyed it beyond use.

Surrounded by fires and walls of burning oil as the USS West Virginia continued to take enemy strafes and bombs, Miller was ready for a fight. Having been raised working with his father and three brothers on a farm, along with being the star halfback on his high school football team, his athleticism and 6'3", 225 lbs build prepared him for what was to come next.

He headed straight for the bridge where he dragged several crew members to safety including Captain Bennion, who was mortally wounded but refused to leave his station. In the face of an onslaught of enemy strafing, bombing, fire, and choking black smoke, he insisted on moving the captain to a safer location.

By then the ship had been hit by two bombs and 6 torpedoes causing the ship to tilt drastically. Miller went with Lt Frederic White to station two which was unmanned with Browning .50-caliber anti-aircraft machine guns. White ordered Miller to start feeding ammo while White fired at incoming Japanese planes. Miller, who was stood on deck covered in oil and water and surrounded by flames, grabbed the second gun, a weapon he had zero training on nor was he allowed to operate as an African American, pulled the trigger, and shot bullets of freedom at the enemy for fifteen minutes before he finally ran out of ammo and was ordered to abandon ship.

The ole girl was sinking. Of course, a ship going down did not stop Miller from continuing to help pull sailors from the burning water. Miller was one of the last three men to abandon the ship as he and his shipmates swam over 300 yards to shore while avoiding more strafing from Japanese planes and patches of flaming oil from the neighboring battleship Arizona. Once on land, Miller continued to help sailors get to safety. He just never stopped serving.

Word spread weeks later in newspapers and radio reports about an unnamed African American hero aboard the ship before Miller was identified on March 14, 1942. Soon, he was celebrated across the country and things got busy for Miller. He was promoted to mess attendant first class, traveled the country promoting war bonds for the military, and his face later appeared on Navy recruiting posters with the caption,   above and beyond the call of duty.

On May 11, 1942, President Roosevelt approved the Navy Cross for Miller, and 16 days later, Admiral Chester Nimitz, Commander in Chief of the Pacific Fleet presented the Navy Cross to Miller aboard the aircraft carrier Enterprise in Pearl Harbor, currently the Navy's highest honor. Miller was the first African American in history to ever receive this award.

He was later reassigned in 1943 aboard the escort carrier USS Liscome Bay. The escort carrier took part in the Battle of Makin which began on November 20th, 1943. Four days in, a Japanese submarine sent a torpedo straight to the stern of the Liscome Bay. She sank into the depths of the ocean within twenty-three minutes taking two-thirds of the
crew, nearly 650 crewmen, including Miller, with her. His unmarked grave lies somewhere off the shores of Gilbert Islands, though his legend lives on. As time has passed, Miller's acts of heroic bravery have been recognized and honored by the naming of schools, parks, and roads along with postage stamps displaying his image.

In 1973, a small and fast warship called a frigate, the USS Miller, was named in his honor. His mother was in attendance.

Interesting facts

- Miller was the USS West Virginia's heavyweight boxing champion, gaining the nickname "Raging Bull."

- Before enlisting in the Navy, Miller wanted to become a taxidermist.

- Miller's actions have been portrayed in the 2001 film Pearl Harbor by actor Cuba Gooding Jr.

- All of Miller's brothers served in WWII

SAMUEL FUQUA

Miller's story onboard the USS West Virginia in the previous chapter was exceptional in his actions along with his resolve to fight an enemy for his country which didn't truly treat him an equal to his white counterparts based on his race.

That said, Miller wasn't the only one who stepped up that day beyond the call of duty nor was the USS West Virginia the only ship hit by the surprise attack from Japan. As you'll soon find out, there were multiple ships attacked and heavily damaged early that Sunday morning and many lives were lost during the battle. These dire circumstances set the stage for true heroes to step up in the first battle to kick off the U.S.'s involvement in the Second World War.

Like Miller, the stories that follow are just a glimpse of the bravery and sacrifice demonstrated that day. Just a small taste of what went on that day. But for those that don't know, you're probably wondering why this all began? Why did Japan target the U.S. naval base stationed at Pearl Harbor in Honolulu, Hawaii?

I'll give you the nutshell version. For roughly 20 years leading up to the attack, tension between Japan and the U.S. had been growing. Within those twenty years, Japan, whose tiny island didn't come with a stack of sweet resources, began to invade China, among other things. The U.S. loaned some cheddar to China so they could purchase war supplies which Japan didn't like.

In 1940, the U.S. stopped the shipments of supplies and parts Japan needed for their conquest, but the U.S. continued to supply oil which Japan was heavily dependent on. In July 1941, the U.S. cut off oil supplies to Japan which they took as a total kick to the nuts. After several failed negotiations between Japan and the U.S., Japan put all their chips on the table. They were all in. A plan was in place to simultaneously attack several locations at once including Guam, the Philippines, Singapore, and Hong Kong. But that came at the risk of U.S. involvement so preventive measures would need to be executed to disrupt a quick naval response from the

U.S. So, they sucker punched us at Pearl Harbor. As you'll later learn from the section of heroes who participated in the Pacific Theatre, we punch back harder.

Which brings us back to December 7, 1941.

Around the same time that the USS West Virginia was hit bringing Doris Miller to his knees in the middle of laundry detail, The USS Arizona, anchored catty cornered to the West Virginia, was also hit. Moments before, Lt. Comdr. Samuel Fuqua, aboard the Arizona, heard the siren alarms while having breakfast in the wardroom, he rushed to the quarter deck.

Hearing the sound of overhead planes, he looked up and saw a bomb falling from the sky. It was heading straight for him. There was no time to react and within a split second, everything went dark. As he came to, the ship he knew that was in working order just moments before was now ablaze. Six feet away was a giant hole left in the wake of the bomb that pierced through several decks before exploding in the captain's pantry. The initial impact blew him back and knocked him unconscious.

Gaining his senses, he looked up and found the midship in flames. Amidst the chaos and panic, Fuqua became a beacon of being calm and collected as he immediately began to direct rescue and fire fighter efforts fulfilling his role as the damage control officer. Moments later an explosion at the forward of the ship sent it in flames as a column of thick black smoke trailed through the air above the ship. The resulting fires were intense and spread rapidly as severely wounded and burned men ran and crawled out onto the deck. The USS Arizona took her fatal blow leaving Fuqua the last living senior officer aboard the ship.

She was going under and heading straight for the harbor floor. Fuqua, operating as if unconcerned from the bombs, enemy strafing, and the charred bodies that littered the ship, continued to direct rescue efforts to get the crew onto the motor launches and boats. Standing knee high in water with a cigar in his mouth, he gave orders like it was just another ordinary day in the Navy. Realizing the ship could not be saved, Fuqua ordered the crew to abandon ship but refused to leave to continue the rescue effort. His unwavering resolve to stay behind encouraged others to do the same.

Fuqua was the last to leave the ship after determining all who could be saved were off the ship. Of all the ships attacked on December 7th, The USS Arizona saw the most casualties with 1177 crew members dying during the battle. Fuqua would receive the Medal of Honor for his efforts aboard the USS Arizona that day.

Interesting Facts

• "Admiral Fuqua's great-great-great-great grandfather was Lieut. William Stark, First Continental Dragoons who fought under General George Washington at Valley Forge, and the Admiral is a member of the Society of the Cincinnati in the State of Virginia."

• Fuqua fought in WWI while in the Army.

PETER TOMICH

Just before the attack initiated on Pearl Harbor, while Doris Miller was working laundry duties and Samuel Fuqua was still eating breakfast aboard their respective ships, a few crew members aboard the USS Utah saw some incoming planes but assumed they were American and went about their day.

The USS Utah was moored off Ford Island away from most of the ships at Pearl Harbor which were located at Battleship Row. The ship had participated in both the Mexican Revolution and WW1. By the end of 1941, she was mainly used for anti-aircraft gunnery training and target practice hit routinely with dummy bombs.

During the attack, some of the Japanese pilots mistook the USS Utah as an aircraft carrier and sent 6 torpedoes its way, two of which made a direct hit causing the ship to take on water. As water quickly rushed into the boiler room below deck like a frightful scene from The Titanic, Chief Watertender Peter Tomich rushed downstairs to the boiler room to warn his crew of their impending doom within the sinking vessel. If nothing was done, those massive boilers would explode in a fire inferno so destructive that no one onboard would survive. If anyone knew those boilers better than anyone, it was Tomich.

Peter Tomich, born in Croatia, immigrated over to the U.S. twenty years previously, shortly before WW1. Tomich joined the Army and served for 18 months though never saw combat. He applied for his citizenship and 10 days after his contract with the Army was up, enlisted with Navy.

He would spend the next 22 years serving in the Navy working his way up to Chief Watertender. With zero family, the Navy and the sailors he worked with day in and day out over two decades became his family. He cherished his crew and their lives above his own which aptly dictated the decision he made that morning the USS Utah as attacked.

Wading through water as the boilers screamed and moaned unimaginable noises, Tomich ordered his crew to get topside and out of harm's way. Within minutes of impact, the Utah was taking in too much water and began to tilt. "Get topside, go....the ship is turning over... you have to escape now," he yelled at them as the water level continued to rise. His crew ran for the stairs and headed for the deck as Tomich, ignoring his own orders, turned in the opposite direction toward the boilers.

At 8:05 am, just a few minutes after the initial attack, the USS Utah was practically on one side at a tilt of 40 degrees. Up top, the sailors who made it onto the deck were met with enemy strafe fire on a ship that was quickly sinking. It was fatal to stay so jumping overboard into the waters and swimming to shore was their only option.

Meanwhile below deck, Tomich, used pipes and rails to stay upright from the ship's tilt. He was busy turning gauges here and there, closing valves, and releasing steam where it was needed to prevent his boilers from becoming a bigger threat to the crew than the enemy flying around outside. Tomich, aware that from the tilt that his time had run out to save himself, continued to work the boilers to save others. He succeeded and the boilers never exploded.

At 8:12 am, the mooring lines snapped as the ship rested on the bottom of the sea floor with part of the hull still sticking out of the water. Tomich went down with the ship at the age of 48 along with 57 others who never made it out whose bodies have never been recovered as they are entombed on the rusty ship to this day. Thanks to the efforts of Tomich, who was awarded the Medal of Honor, hundreds of men were given time to escape and to see another day.

With no next of kin, Tomich's Medal of Honor went unclaimed for decades. And it looked to always go unclaimed if it weren't for the work of one man.

Robert "Bob" Lunney, 17 at the time, saw firsthand the carnage of the aftermath at Pearl Harbor after the attack. The site had a lasting impression on him as a young sailor, especially of the sunken USS Utah and the story of Tomich who gave his life to save others. Lunney went on to fight in WWII as a sailor and in the Korean War as a Merchant Marine. Later in life as the story of Tomich stuck with him all those years, in 1997, Lunney started a nine-year journey to find Tomich's next of kin. After years of research, digging through archives, and jumping through hoops, Lunney made a trip to Croatia to the village Tomich was born and found a distant cousin. In 2006, Tomich's Medal of Honor was presented to his family members aboard the USS Enterprise.

Interesting Facts

- There is a document of the heroic acts of Peter Tomich called Heroes are Never Forgotten - A Peter Tomich Story

- Peter Tomich came over to the U.S. with his cousin, John Tonic, who he put down as his emergency contact information when he originally enlisted. The military were not aware that John had moved back to Croatia years before WW2 when they tried to reach out to Peter's next of kin to receive the Medal of Honor on Peter's behalf.

GEORGE WELCH AND KENNETH TAYLOR

The night before the attack on Pearl Harbor, brand new officers George Welch, 23, and Kenneth Taylor, 21, were both living it up and looking fresh in their tuxedos as they danced the night away at the Officer's Club. This was a weekly occurrence for these two young pilots stationed in Hawaii. The club would open at 9 pm and the dancing wouldn't stop until daybreak. And with the next day being Sunday, an off-duty day, both Welch and Taylor didn't object when after an entire night at the club, a poker game started into the wee hours of the morning.

At 6:30 am, after the last winner of the hand counted their chips, Welch and Taylor decided to call it a night to get some shut eye on their day off. Little did they know that their shut eye would be cut short.

At 7:55 am, both Welch and Taylor were awakened by the sound of explosions. Throwing on the closest clothes nearby, they both donned some of their tuxedos before running out of their respective rooms and outside. Alerted by the site of Japanese planes and flames off in the distance, Taylor called the ground crews at Haleiwa to ready their planes while Welch grabbed Taylor's car before speeding off towards Haleiwa.

Topping speeds at 100 mph, they quickly traversed the 10 miles between Wheeler and the Haleiwa air strip. Strapping into their planes, and after being told the only fire power on

the P-40 was 30 caliber ammunition, both pilots pushed full throttle and zipped down the runway ready to fight. In the air, both Welch and Taylor took out Japanese planes and successfully dispersed a group of enemy fighters before running out of ammo.

Both landed at Wheeler to reload within minutes of each other as ground crews approached their planes only to tell them that orders came in to stay on the ground. After arguing with Welch who was resolved to keep fighting, the ground crew servicing his vehicle gave up and loaded him up with .50 caliber rounds. The crew working with Taylor, seeing the results of the other crew with Welch, didn't even try to argue and simply loaded .50 caliber rounds into his plane.

Welch took off back into the fight as the roar from another wave of enemy planes approached their location. The ground crew, not quite done loading ammunition into Taylor's plane, ran for cover leaving Taylor in his plane. In his way was an armament dolly left by the ground crew. Left with few options, he punched the throttle as his plane ran it over and was in the air back in the fight.

While in the air, Taylor estimated the location of the enemy formation but couldn't quite see through the smoke and clouds. When he thought he was trailing behind them in position to strike, when in fact he was in the middle of their formation. Next came a hail of fire from Japanese bullets one which went through his arm and another sending shrapnel into his leg.

Welch, who was able to see Taylor's dire situation, was able to descend on the enemy plane and return fire with his .50 caliber ammunition nailing a direct hit sending the plane down in flames toward the island. Taylor, out of immediate threat, rolled out of the formation and repositioned at the rear of the formation and took out the plane in the tail end before heading back to Wheeler to disrupt another formation of Japanese planes before running out of ammunition a second time.

By the end of battle when the remaining Japanese forces had retreated and both Welch and Taylor had landed safely, combined they took out 6 Japanese planes with two more probables during their two sorties solidifying their mark in history as the first to see air combat during the war though still not officially declared at the time. Welch was expected to be put up for the Medal of Honor but was denied because Welch and Taylor had taken off without orders.

Interesting Facts

- After the battle, both Taylor and Welch ran into their squadron commander who thought, based on their attire, that they had goofed off during the entire battle.

- Though a controversial topic, it is believed that Welch broke the sound barrier first on October 1, 1947 and again on October 14, just a few minutes before Chuck Yeager

- Both pilots would go on to participate in the war. Welch, for example, would fly a total of 348 combat missions and land 16 confirmed kills.

- George Welch was actually born George Louis Schwartz, Jr. but due to anti-German prejudice at the time during WW1, his parents decided to change George's and his brother's last name to Welch, his mother's maiden name.

- Welch died in an unfortunate accident during a F-100A demonstration flight in 1954.

Only **139** cars were manufactured in the US during the war.

JOHN FINN

Lying in bed, debating with his wife as to who would make the morning coffee, was Chief Petty Officer John Finn stationed at Naval Air Station Kaneohe Bay, Hawaii. On his well-earned off day, work, duty, and service were far from his thoughts of things he thought he'd do that day. With caffeine on his mind early that Sunday morning, both Finn and his wife could hear the distant sound of low-flying planes and gun fire.

Living within brand spanking new barracks that didn't even have curtains yet, Finn could see flames and smoke in the distance as he was beginning to realize something wasn't right. Noticing the planes flying were single engine while theirs on the island had multiple engines, things didn't add up especially when the sound of machine gun fire didn't register as friendly. If there was any question as to whether something might be wrong, a knock on the door from his neighbor letting him know he was needed down at the squadron right away pretty much sealed the deal.

Understanding the emergency, he grabbed his chief hat, bolted out the door, cranked his vehicle, and screamed down the road a whopping…20 mile per hour. Apparently, no emergency is too great to ruin a perfect driving reputation. That was until a low flying plane came just overhead from his rear giving Finn a good view of the big red "meatball" on the wings of the plane. It was definitely not one of theirs. They were Japanese and no doubt were conducting an all-out assault. Finn put his car into second and surprised himself when he didn't run anyone over making his way to the hanger.

Once he arrived, he found his men with .30 and .50 caliber machine guns firing from the door of the hanger. Finn grabbed a .50 caliber machine gun from the squadron painter, attached it to a movable platform used for training, and rolled it outside about 25 yards from the hanger in plain view to send those Japanese fighters a warm welcome. For two hours straight, he sent buckets of bullets into the skies aiming at every single enemy plane that got near him. In some cases, the planes got so close he could see the Japanese faces as they flew by.

Of course, targeting enemy planes also made him a bit of a target as well as he withstood enemy strafing and endured 21 wounds in the process all the while sending fire his weapon and coordinating his crew's defensive maneuvers. As he put it, I didn't have enough sense to come in out of the rain. Only when ordered to get medical treatment did he get looked at only to receive minimum care before returning to his squadron to help arm the surviving American planes.

For his efforts, Finn would be the first to be awarded the Medal of Honor in WW2. He was awarded the Medal of Honor aboard the USS Enterprise though not the same USS Enterprise that the Medal of Honor was presented to Peter Tomich's family in 2006.
`

Interesting Facts

- The first time Finn met a standing president was when he was 100 years old.

- Before he died, Finn was the last living Medal of Honor recipient from Pearl Harbor.

GEORGE WALTERS

Just before the raid by Japan, while most of the ships were stationed on water, the USS Pennsylvania was dry docked with two other destroyers Cassin and Downes. In the drydock, all three ships were at a huge handicap that would go unnoticed until just shy of 8 am that morning when a normal day at the dock turned into a battlefield.

Within the confines of the drydock, which acted like a box for the ships to sit in, it was difficult to see over the walls of the deck for the crew members onboard. As the attack was just beginning, the crew had no idea what was happening. They were moving along as if it was business as usual. Lucky for them, they had a man with a bird's eye view who saw it all. George Walters, sitting 50 ft off the ground in his crane beside the dock, saw the first planes diving on Ford Island. Thinking it was a drill, he thought nothing of it. That was until explosions, fires, and pillars of black smoke gave him the realization that this was no drill. Their island was under attack.

Walter looked down at the crew members on the USS Pennsylvania completely clueless of the dire situation around them. Walter tried yelling but they couldn't hear him. So, what was a crane operator to do in a situation like that? He threw a wrench down at them. That got their attention, but it only served to piss them off. They looked up only to see Walter violently mouthing some words and frantically waving his arms around. They probably thought the crane operator had lost his marbles.

As the attack continued to spread, the crew finally got the message. The air defense alarms went off and condition "YOKE" was put in place which basically meant to the entire ship, it was go time. The crew were quick to respond, breaking locks off ammunition ready boxes and they manned battle stations ready to return fire. But again, the walls of the dock made it difficult to see where the planes were coming from before they were right on top of them.

Walter, using the arm of his crane, pointed in the direction of the oncoming enemy formations so the crew below could be ready to fire in the right direction. Thanks to this crane operator, it was officially yoke'n time. Walter then used his giant metal crane moving it back and forth over the USS Pennsylvania making it more difficult for low-flying Japanese planes to get close to the drydocked ship.

Walter continued his defensive efforts for over an hour before Japan dropped a 500 lb bomb close to his crane. It was a near miss and caused a seventeen-foot crater. The explosion knocked Walter completely unconscious and almost out of the crane, but he managed to survive. Though not a soldier, sailor, or marine, Walter was nonetheless a hero that day and the USS Pennsylvania made it out with minimum damage.

Interesting Facts

- Lewis Walter, George's son, worked on Navy vessels during the Vietnam War and was captured. He was held for three days and tortured as sharp bamboo sticks were jabbed into his legs to keep him from escaping.

- The USS Pennsylvania ended its lengthy career with a bang. A literal one. From a nuke. Two nukes actually. Ole girl was blasted twice in 1946 during nuclear testing at Bikini Atoll.

The British soldiers' ration of
toilet paper during the war was

3

sheets per day.

The US soldiers received

22.

EDWIN HILL

The same morning John Finn tried his best to convince his wife to make a cup of joe and while George Welch and Kenneth Taylor were catching an hour's sleep after a long night of dancing and poker, the crew onboard the USS Nevada were carrying out the orders of the day. The USS Nevada was moored on Battleship Row along with several other ships that morning with a light schedule of events for the day. But what should have been a boring and relaxing Sunday quickly became a hotbed of nasty as the Japanese Imperial Navy sent out fighters to donkey kick the US Naval Fleet stationed at Pearl Harbor.

As the attack was underway on Ford Island and George Walters was busy throwing wrenches at sailors to get their attention, Chief Boatswain Edwin Hill was onboard the USS Nevada doing his thing that morning when a torpedo struck the hull of his ship. The hull held steady, but the joints couldn't withstand it. They leaked water as the damage control team ran to the scene to do whatever they could to fix it, wondering what in Uncle Sam's name just hit the boat. Though there wasn't a second to think because Japan was heading with their second wave of fighters to drop 500 lb dumps on Battleship Row.

After seeing the USS Arizona take giant bomb turd to the face so large that it would make you drop a bomb of your own in your trousers, the commander of the Nevada wasn't going to stick around to be next. The commander of the ship, with a clear opening to get the hell out of there, decided to make a run for the sea. But there was one problem. The ship was moored to the dock with some stupid heavy ropes
called hawsers. These jokers are as thick as a man's head, and someone was going to have to untie from the dock or the ship was going to continue to be target practice for the Japanese. But then there was another problem. There was no one on the dock to do it.

Both landed at Wheeler to reload within minutes of each other as ground crews approached their planes only to tell them that orders came in to stay on the ground. After arguing with Welch who was resolved to keep fighting, the ground crew servicing his vehicle gave up and loaded him up with .50 caliber rounds. The crew working with Taylor, seeing the results of the other crew with Welch, didn't even try to argue and simply loaded .50 caliber rounds into his plane.

There was no battle plan or protocol for getting completely wrecked by an enemy force unexpectedly on your own turf. Hill took matters into his own hands and did an Olympic 10 out of 10 swan dive off the ship into the harbor. He swam to the docks and set the USS Nevada free by man handling those heavy ropes. He successfully set her free but then she was on the move, with him still on the dock.

He sprinted off the dock and jumped right back into the harbor chasing after the boat. He was literally swimming to war about the same time Samuel Fuqua was onboard the blazing USS Arizona giving orders in between puffs of his cigar. Hill somehow managed to catch up to the battleship high tailing it into sea and then pulled himself into the deck probably using the crusty barnacles as leverage.
Back on deck, he was soaked but there was no time for high fives. He had literal fires to put out and people to lead as they headed away from the harbor.

The escape caught the eye of the Japanese as a formation of 23 fighters zeroed in on their location as they were the only ship to escape. Meanwhile the anti-aircraft weapons on board were busy screaming constant streams of piercing metal. Some of them made their mark but there were just too many heading their way. Enemy fire strafed the starting fires and killed several causing the ship to practically limp away from danger. The commander, thinking that any more damage could cause the ship to sink, decided to run the ship to shore before that could happen. He needed the anchored dropped to finish the job.

Hill was there ready to do the job and in position to release the anchor when a bomb struck the ship and several other ships nearby. It blew Hill off the ship and killed him ending his service to his country, but not until after going down a legend. For his efforts, he was posthumously awarded the Medal of Honor. Not to mention, the USS Nevada would go on to fight in the war and wreck some carnage blasting the beaches of Normandy on D-Day saving countless lives.

FUN FACT

AFTER THE ATTACK ON PEARL HARBOR, PRESIDENT ROOSEVELT USED AL CAPONE'S LIMO AS A BULLET PROOF VEHICLE WHICH HAD BEEN SEIZED AFTER HIS ARREST FOR TAX EVASION.

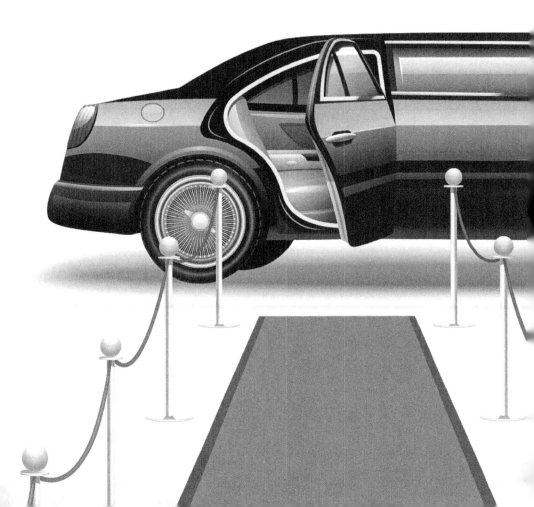

PHIL RASMUSSEN

On the morning of the attack, George Welch and Kenneth Taylor were not the only two young pilots to go to bed in peace yet wake up to battle. Another pilot, still in his purple pajamas, saw the carnage underway while he was taking his early morning piss.

The day before on December 6, 1941, the Army Air Core unit stationed at Wheeler Field performed the long tedious task of inspecting every plane and parking them wingtip-to-wingtip. After a long morning of inspections, Lt Phil Rasmussen and another pilot quickly exited Wheeler Field to pick up their dates 30 minutes away at Honolulu for a night of drinks, body surfing, and music only heading back to the barracks after dropping off the girls at 2 am, December 7th. On the ride back to Wheeler Field, the road passed high above Pearl Harbor. Rasmussen got a panoramic view of the whole harbor and the sleeping fleet down below lit up from stem to stern. Nudging his friend who had started snoozing in the passenger seat, he asked, "Did you ever see so many lights at Pearl Harbor?" Barely waking up, his friend answered, "What a target that would make." Prophetic words.

6 hours later, through the latrine window, Rasmussen could see planes off in the distance at the flight line roughly 300 yards away, drop an object, which left a fireball explosion upon impact. At first, he thought the Navy was up to some realistic tricks. Often the Army Air Corps would drop flour "bombs" on the Navy as a prank and the Navy would reciprocate. This was not one of

those times. As the plane pulled away, he could see the red meatball on the side of the plane.

He immediately yelled down the hall to the others within the barracks that they were being attacked by Japs. With no time to think, he ran back to his room in the barracks, grabbed his shows, belt, and his .45 pistol before running out the door to enter the fight.

Just outside the flight line, he hid behind a palm plant as he took shots at the Japanese flying by as they strafed. Approaching the flight line still wearing his purple pajamas, he saw the area in chaos. Ammunition was exploding in the hangers and fires were everywhere, as hostile planes flew in low strafing the planes parked wingtip-to-wingtip. As one exploded and caught fire, the one next to it did the same in a destructive chain caused from them being so close together.

Luckily, there were still some undamaged Curtis P-36 Hawks further away. They were older but what other options were there? Rasmussen ran down and strapped in one along with 3 other pilots, loaded up ammunition, and took off while receiving enemy fire. The 23-year-old officer was one of very few pilots to get airborne during the surprise attack.

While gaining altitude, he pulled a lever to arm his weapons. Once he pulled the lever and released it, the .50 caliber started firing by itself. When he charged the .30 caliber, it wouldn't fire at all. To save ammunition, he had to disengage the lever until the time was right.

Their first orders were to head to Kaneohe Bay, the same area John Finn first saw the attack from his window. At about 900 feet, they could see dive bombers attacking Kaneohe Bay, so they dove in to disperse the enemy. There, he ran into 11 Japanese Zeros, far superior planes compared to his lemon P-36. He was heavily outnumbered as he entered the dogfight.

He released the lever to charge the .50 caliber gun which began to fire by itself again. Lucky for him, one of the meatball fighters happened to fly directly in the line of his fire taking it out. As he pulled up, two enemy Zeroes double teamed him. One tried to ram after his Zero ran out of ammunition and was experiencing engine failure. As Rasmussen pulled away to dodge him, the other Zero pilot unloaded their weapon into his P-36.

450 bullets holes later, the two Zeroes had taken out his tail wheel, his rudder control, his hydraulic controls and caused the canopy of his plane to shatter. All hell had broken loose. His plane shuddering from the onslaught and covered in his canopy's plexi glass, managed to find refuge in a well-placed cloud below as he tried to gain back control of his plane.

One he leveled out, he reached to feel the top of his head convinced part of it was missing during the altercations. Feeling a head full of hair and just some plexi glass, he was good to go. Now he just had to land... without a back wheel... or brakes... while receiving friendly fire... from friendly ground forces who were shooting at anything that flew...wearing nothing but purple pajamas... Piece of cake.

He would have to land at Wheeler Field which didn't have an actual runway. Just a grass field still wet from the morning dew. Somehow the young LT pulled it off and managed to land the plane at Wheeler Field earning himself the Silver Star. As the adrenaline gradually faded, he looked around while still in his cockpit at the burning hangers and the smoke rising from rows of damaged planes as fear entered the equation for the first time. He looked down at this watch. Fifty minutes from takeoff. Shaken, he got out of the plane and walked back to the barracks to change out of his sweat soaked pajamas, traded them for a flight suit, and went back to the flight line.

Even with the bravery and guts of men like Rasmussen, the others we've already covered, among the countless others, the attack on Pearl Harbor was still a devastating blow that took the country by surprise. The losses were heavy and mind blowing with 2,403 dead and 1,178 wounded within two hours. Not to mentioned 118 American planes were completed destroyed, many more damaged, and the Oklahoma, West Virginia, Arizona, and California battleships of the fleet either sunk to the harbor floor or were completely beyond repair. The sucker punch might have knocked us down but didn't keep us down as even more brave men stood up to answer the nations call to punch right back.

Interesting Facts

• There is a display at the National Museum of the Air Force in Dayton, Ohio that features a mannequin of Lt Phil Rasmussen scrambling into a P-36 plane wearing his pajamas. The display has been dubbed "The Pajama Pilot." (3)

• The Japanese pilot who tried ramming Rasmussen who was experiencing engine failure didn't think he could make it back to the carrier, so he decided to take someone down with him, mainly Rasmussen. Somehow, he managed to make it back to the carrier.

CHAPTER 2:
PACIFIC THEATRE
HEROES

"All wars are civil wars, because all men are brothers."
~ Francois Fenelon

JOHN BASILONE PART 1

Months after Japan jacked up Pearl Harbor and during the same month Japan kicked some serious US tail out of the Philippines, Japanese forces invaded Guadalcanal.

The Guadalcanal is just off the coast of Australia and is a lovely place to visit if you love dense tropical jungles, carrying around machetes everywhere you go, and malaria. Just a lovely disease-ridden tropical paradise if there ever was one. But why would Japan want possession of this dump island far away from the mainland?

Japan's island conquest, along with several others, was an attempt to build a protective ring of islands around Japan that served to hinder communication and supply chains between Australia, New Zealand, and the US. Not to mentioned Japan's little ole island didn't have many resources to begin with, so they were on the hunt of taking resources from anyone and everyone close by which put Guadalcanal on the map.

The US, needing to stop Japan's relentless expansion and control the sea line communication between Australia and the US launched the first amphibious landing in the war on 7 August 1942 in hopes of claiming the island and the airfield being constructed by Japanese forces.

This battle over land, sea, and air resulted in US forces, mainly made up of the Marine Corp and the Navy, along with Australian and New Zealand forces, taking control of the island and the airfield being constructed at Lunga Point quickly. Defending the airfield, on the other hand, is where the real battle began which would come to be known as the Battle of Henderson Field.

Fully aware of the strategic importance of Guadalcanal, Japan sent 15,000 troops on October 23, 1942 to overwhelm the Allied forces in a fierce countermeasure to take it back.

On October 24th, Sgt John Basilone was defending the line about 1,000 yards south of Henderson Field at the Lunga Ridge. Among torrents of rain creating what seemed like bottomless mud in the tropical arena, Basilone, a Marine Section leader, was in charge of two heavy .30-caliber machine gun sections and roughly 16 men as they would soon challenge wave after wave of Japanese forces stacked with grenades, small arms and machine guns of their own. Their task: defend a narrow pass at the Tenaru River.

As the small crew dug in for the night in their gun pits caked in mud and after already defending their position since the beginning of the battle on the 23rd, 3,000 enemy combatants attacked the line. The first wave taken out, merely acted as a bridge over flesh-shredding barbed wire so future waves could pass through. This enemy was savagely determined to win. Against the odds, Basilone fought valiantly with his malaria-ridden men as man and machine were tested to their very limits. Through countless waves, explosions, and heavy fire resulting in casualties on both sides, the Japanese forces were being kept at bay but one of the gun crews were disabled by enemy fire.

Eventually left with only two other men and without any regard for his own life, Basilone picked up a 90-pound machine gun, tripod, and ammunition and ran across 200 yards under continual fire to the silenced gun section. Along the route he encountered Japanese soldiers who

he killed with his Colt .45 pistol before reaching his destination. Once in the pit, he hastily setup shop to fire point blank at the charging Japanese. A second later and he would have been the one overtaken.

Throughout the night, Basilone would repeatedly repair guns jammed with mud and water and change out scalding hot barrels in almost total darkness for his junior Marines. At one point, he lost his asbestos gloves which were critical for holding or manning heavily used machine guns. Without hesitation, Basilone continued to barehand the searing barrels of his machine gun to continuously pound buckets of steel downrange obliterating an entire wave of incoming soldiers burning his hands and arms in the process.

Enemy bodies were literally stacking up into a wall that Basilone and his men would periodically have to leave their defensive position to knock over just to reestablish their clear field of fire in preparation for the next wave that never seemed to end.

Later in the night, as ammo, moral, and able-bodied marines were running low along with enemy forces attacking from the rear disrupting his supply lines, Basilone dashed across 200 yards again through heavy fire to an ammunition point to gather much needed supplies for his men before dashing back. This trip he would not just make once but twice to keep his men in the fight. As ammo ran out and just before dawn, wielding nothing but his pistol and a machete, Basilone, exhausted, caked in mud and sweat, continued to fight, and defend the line until reinforcements finally arrived.

Nash Phillips, who lost his hand while fighting with Basilone, was receiving medical treatment when he got a visit from his Sergeant. Phillips described him as, "barefooted and his eyes were red as fire. His face was dirty black from gunfire and lack of sleep. His shirt sleeves were rolled up to his shoulders. He had a .45 tucked into the waistband of his trousers. He'd just dropped by to see how I was making out; me and the others in the section. I'll never forget him. "Which begs the question...did our boy, Basilone, lose his shoes during battle?? How hard do you have to put out that your boots don't even make it out alive? I can only imagine that at some point it was easier to maneuver through the mud without them.

The largest tank battle during the war and in history involved

3,600 tanks

between Germany and Russia.

The battle waged on for six months but the Japanese evacuated Guadalcanal in February of 1943. In the end, Basilone, age 26, was accredited with killing 38 Japanese and awarded the Medal of Honor for his efforts. He would later be shipped back home a celebrated war hero, but his acts of valor were not over and neither was his story...

Interesting Facts

- Originally joined the Army and was stationed in the Philippines where became a boxing champion. This is where he got the nickname "Manila John" Basilone.

- Henderson field was named after Major Lofton Henderson, the first Marine aviator to perish during the Battle of Midway.

MITCHEL PAIGE

Three days after John Basilone's stand against waves of Japanese troops at the Lunga Ridge, another Marine found himself practically alone fighting off close to 2,500 hostile troops holding the line at Henderson Field after his entire unit of thirty-six men had been either injured or killed in action.

The night before on October 25, 1942, Marine Platoon Leader Mitchel Paige was hunkered down for the night in foxholes with the rest of his men when off in the thick jungle he could see lights flickering in the distance. One of his men called him over to their foxhole thinking he was hallucinating seeing random light in the distance. He wasn't. They were Japanese troops close by who had infiltrated their territory under the cover of darkness. They were using the lights to send singles amongst themselves. Paige, as quietly as he could, crawled over to his men's positions to train their eyes toward the enemy and to hold their fire.

There was a big issue with Marines who were way too trigger happy especially at night when brush vegetation moving in the wind appeared to be hostile troops camouflaged among the jungle. Thousands of countless rounds were lost on shadows. In this case, Paige and his men were not facing shadows but Japanese troops way too close for comfort. Firing would have been the natural reaction but would have given away their position too soon. Earlier, Paige and his men had set up a tripwire with field ration cans attached to it that would rattle if anyone hit the wire.

As the hours passed that felt like years, the enemy force encroached closer as Paige could hear their voices nearby. Paige held a grenade in his hand with the pin already drawn as several of his men had already done the same.

At 0200 in the morning on October 26th, an eerie silence filled the darkness as Paige could even hear his men breathing yards away. A Japanese soldier tripped the wire causing the food ration cans to rattle. Someone shrieked and all hell broke loose. Japanese machine gun fire sprayed in all directions peppering the jungle as grenades exploded all around them. Over the immense gun fire and explosion, Paige and his men could hear the enemy screaming, "Banzai!" and "Blood for the Emperor!" in which the Marines replied, "Blood for Eleanor!" as a tribute to President Roosevelt's wife.

After the first wave of American grenades went off, a swarm of Japanese soldiers rushed toward their position when Paige finally gave the order to fire. Machine guns rattled the night air as 75 hostile troops attacked from all sides with small arms, bayonets and Japanese officers swinging samurai swords of all things during the assault. And then...they vanished. After taking out several of his men and wounding others, they were gone.

Paige tried to get accountability and repair a machine gun when a second assault more successful than the first decimated what was left of his unit leaving him alone to fight them off. Running in the dark from machine gun to machine gun, he fired round after round into enemy forces hoping to send a message that he wasn't alone.

It was getting close to dawn and Paige knew that if he didn't do whatever he could to drive back the hostile forces soon, daybreak would reveal to the Japanese just how much ground they had gained into US territory. To his horror, he saw enemy forces heading straight for one of his machine guns completely out in the open and unmanned. Literally racing a Japanese soldier, who also wanted hands on the weaponry, he traversed through jungle terrain as he dodged enemy fire and snipers hiding in trees managing to reach it first only to find it unloaded.

The enemy racing him dropped 25 yards away and unloaded a 30-round magazine aiming straight for his neck all the while missing every shot. Paige could feel the heat from the bullets zipping between the bottom of his chin and his chest just in front of his Adam's apple. As the last bullet left the enemy's gun barrel, Paige loaded his and fired his gun. Unlike the enemy, he did not miss.

At around 0530, dawn had broken as a ragtag group of men had shown up as reinforcements. Paige, filled with a second wind to continue the fight, instructed them to follow him with their bayonets after the enemy during their retreat. Paige, armed with an 80 lb machine gun with zero protection for his hand on the scalding hot barrel, led the charge. But the battle was over, and that same eerie silence fell over the jungle just as it did at 0200 that morning before the battle began. Paige took a moment to soak in the panoramic view of the island in front of him and thought to himself if it weren't for the hundreds of bodies littered among the jungle floor, what a beautiful place it was.

In 1936, when Paige set off to enlist, his mother gave him parting words from scripture. Years later, after the bloody battle he fought in 1942, he found himself in a foxhole covered in blood, sweat, and wounds that needed attention after chasing off the Japanese force. He emptied his pack looking for something, other than dirt, to pack his wounds. Of the items that fell out of his sack was a bible turned to the page of his mother's words, Proverbs 3:5-6, "Trust in the Lord with all your heart and lean not on your own understanding, in all your ways acknowledge Him and He will direct your paths."

For his efforts, Paige was awarded the Medal of Honor.

Interesting Facts

- Paige passed away in 2003 at the age of 85. He was the last living Medal of Honor recipient during the Guadalcanal Campaign.

- Paige several years after the war wrote a book about his time during WW2.

- Paige walked 200 miles to the closest recruiting station to enlist in the Marine Corps.

THOMAS A. BAKER

In the summer of 1944, Operation Forager, was put into place to launch an offensive attack against the Imperial Japanese forces in the Mariana Islands and Palau. The Mariana Islands are a 750-kilometer strip of islands located in the Pacific Ocean that just so happened to be prime real estate for the war effort.

Commander Chester Nimitz, Commander in Chief of the US Pacific Fleet, wanted the Mariana Islands and he wanted them bad. Let's face it, the US needed it to end the war. Liberating the islands of the Japanese forces would not only allow a strategic location to retake the Philippines but would also allow the US to be within range for B-29 Superfortress bombers to target Japan.

One of the islands of particular interest was the island of Saipan which is located just north of the island of Tinian, the departure location for the nuclear attacks on Japan.

The invasion of US forces into Saipan began on 13 June 1944 and would be referred to as "Pacific D-Day."Troops wouldn't actually get boots on the shores of the island until 0700 two days later on 15 June. Even with strategically placed barbed wire, artillery, trenches, and machine gun emplacements, by nightfall, US troops had secured 6 miles wide of the beachfront to progress the invasion.

Surprised by the attack, the Imperial Japanese Navy tried to counter US Navy forces at sea but were obliterated at the loss of three aircraft carriers and hundreds of planes. The heavy losses resulted in the loss of resupply and reinforcements which made them sitting ducks. Sucks to suck. However, these ducks were not going to go out without a fight. Japanese forces had all but lost the island except for Mount Tapochau where battles in this rough terrain would be nicknamed "Hell's Pocket" among others. This was a nasty place to advance to say the least.

By early July, the Japanese had nowhere to retreat and, as a last-ditch effort, made plans for a final suicidal banzai charge as one method of honorable suicide. Of the 29,000 Japanese troops that occupied the inland before the invasion, roughly 4300 were left for this final Hail Mary as they charged into battle as one giant unit until the last man was standing.

Two weeks prior to this bloody battle, the craziest man on the island had stepped into the scene wreaking havoc literally everywhere he went. This man was none other than Private Thomas A. Baker.

Baker grew up in Troy, New York and enlisted with the Army soon after graduating high school. He found himself in Company A, in the 105th Infantry Regiment, 27th Infantry Division. Believe me when I tell you this soldier could have been in a division all on his own. He was practically the Saipan Boogie Man, and you'll soon realize why.

On 19 June, Private Baker and his company found themselves under heavy fire by a Japanese emplacement that wanted nothing more than to turn US troops into bullet sponges. Baker was going to have none of that. While most would duck and cover and call-in reinforcements, Baker lived by the beat of a different drum. That drum being a bazooka he borrowed from a comrade before walking out into the battlefield, kneeling down on one knee 100 yards from the enemy while under fire, and knocking out a strategic strongpoint with not the first round, but the second. He then walked, not ran, but walked back to his company with bullets flying all around him.

He had nerves of steel, and Baker wasn't done at that point. A few days later, during his company's advancement, Baker took up the rear to protect against surprise attacks and stumbled upon two heavily fortified pockets manned by 12 enemy forces. What was Baker to do other than kill all of them single handedly? And that's exactly what he did. Not bad for a day's work. 500-yards farther, he found six more enemy forces and, according to his Medal of Honor citation which I believe says it best, "destroyed all of them." He was literally a force not to be reckoned with.

Now back to those Banzai attacks. On July 7th, Baker found himself in a foxhole during the largest Banzai attacks of the Battle of Saipan from anywhere between 3000 to 5000 men. He unloaded his M1 until the enemy was within 5 yards of his position and he was completely out of ammo. No worries, Baker would resort to using his M1 as a baseball bat to beat down a dozen or more Japanese attackers.

At some point he was struck in the stomach but refused to evacuate because who needs a stomach when you have a fist for hand-to-hand combat. He was eventually hit again and began to bleed out as a comrade dragged him 50 yards before he himself was hit. Not wanting to be the reason his fellow men were injured he demanded to be left behind telling another soldier to, Get the hell away from me. I've caused enough problems. Gimme your .45. Baker had no intention of being rescued if it meant putting others at risk. He was last seen alive propped against a tree with a single gun loaded with 8 bullets.

The next day when his comrades gained back the advance, they found Baker dead at the age of 28, still propped up against the same tree, his gun empty, and eight Japanese soldiers dead in his vicinity. On 9 July, a day after he was found, US forces took control of the entire island. Though Baker never lived to leave Saipan alive, he made sure plenty of Japanese forces didn't either. He was posthumously awarded the Medal of Honor.

BEN L. SALOMON

In the exact same unit that Thomas Baker was in, the 27th Infantry Division, was another Medal of Honor recipient though this soldier was not sent to the front lines. This hero was sent to war...to be a dentist.

On the same day, July 7th, that Baker was busy manning the front line, Capt. Salomon was manning the rear, taking names, and pulling teeth. Or at least that's what a typical dentist would be up to. Not Salomon.

A few years back when Salomon graduated Southern California's dental program, he tried enlisting with both the U.S. and Canadian armies in 1937. Apparently, Salomon, who came from a Jewish background, didn't like how his Jewish brothers and sisters were being treated by the invading Germany. He was denied by both militaries and decided to open his own dental practice.

Eventually, he was drafted as a private into the U.S. Army and quickly proved himself as a killer marksman and a top-tier machine gunner. He was born for the front lines, but the Army had different plans. After hearing that Salomon was a dentist, the Army offered him a commission to become a military dentist. Salomon, thinking this was an offer you could refuse, turned down the opportunity to stay with his unit as a gunner. The Army laughed. The "offer" became an order and he soon commissioned into the dental corps. The only battle he would see was with cavities and gingivitis...if he was a normal dentist.

Within his unit, he cleaned teeth in the morning and voluntarily instructed soldiers at night. He also participated in physical training with his unit which was unheard of for medical personnel. He was called the "best all-around soldier" in his unit and was promoted to Captain a month before he'd see combat.

As the 27th was in full swing attacking the shores of Saipan, Salomon was in full swing boredom offshore. Apparently, there are not a lot of teeth that needed attention in the middle of battle. Word got around that the 2nd Battalion's surgeon had been wounded, and Salomon jumped at the opportunity to replace him. His wish was granted. Salomon was soon ashore working a medical tent triage barely 50 yards from the front line and only 30 yards from the shore on July 7th, the second day of the Japanese suicide banzai chargers.

The Japanese were instructed to die honorably and kill at least 10 US soldiers before dying. These were the same attacks where Baker found himself surrounded on three sides as he returned fire from his fox hole before using his weapon as a bat.

The combat at the front was fierce and relentless as the casualties ran high within minutes as 3000 to 5000 hostile troops fell upon the front lines at 0500. Salomon found himself caring for 30 wounded soldiers within his aide tent with plenty more waiting outside to be treated when the enemy pierced through the trench line.

Through the chaos inside the tent, Salomon noticed a Japanese soldier rushed from the brush and started stabbing wounded soldiers who were laid near the tent, with a bayonet. This of course sounds pretty messed up but when you remember these enemy troops were given zero hope of survival and a quota, it makes sense.

Salomon picked up a rifle, squatted down, and took him out. Before he could continue giving aid to the wounded, two others burst through the front entrance of the tent. Close by, Salomon swung his rifle like a bat, clubbed the first one and hit the other with the butt end of his rifle before shooting one and bayonetting the other. The enemy, realizing the front entrances were a no-go, decided to make their own entrance as four Japanese soldiers crawled under the walls of the tent.

Salomon, quick to react, stabbed one, shot another with his last bullet, and bayoneted the third. The fourth, on the other hand, was not going to go down without a fight. Salomon butted the fourth in the stomach before beginning hand-to-hand combat. A wounded soldier lying on a bed pulled out his gun and shot the fourth invader.

Salomon, realizing the dire situation, ordered everyone to evacuate while he stayed behind to cover their retreat. He was last heard saying, "I'll hold them off until you get them to safety. See you later." He ran outside the front entrance of the tent and took over the machine gun after four other soldiers manning it before him were killed. He would go on to receive 24 bullet wounds as he continued to move positions further back to hold back waves of hostile forces.

15 hours passed before friendly forces could finish off the last of the banzai charge and make it back to his position. He was found slumped over the machine gun having received 76 bullet and bayonet wounds, finger still on the trigger, and 98 enemy forces lying dead before him. Capt. Salomon would go on to receive the Medal of Honor for his war efforts.

Interesting Facts

• Salomon was one of only three dentists to ever receive the Medal of Honor.

• Salomon did actually receive the medal until 2002. At first, his medal recommendation was rejected because the Geneva Convention prohibited medical personnel from bearing arms against enemy forces. It was later ruled that actions in defense are not prohibited just as in the case for Capt. Salomon.

AMERICANS USED THE NAME

'LIBERTY STEAK'

INSTEAD OF

'HAMBURGER'

BECAUSE IT WAS TOO GERMAN SOUNDING.

ROBERT B. NETT

As the Pacific campaign was well underway, in March of 1944, General Douglas MacArthur, who vowed to return to liberate the Philippines after Japan kicked Allied forces out back in 1942, was given orders to retake the Philippines starting with the Island of Leyte under the operation codenamed King Two. Allied forces would have to battle roughly 20,000 Japanese troops during monsoon season...Yay...

Operation to invade Leyte began on 17 October 1944 as Rangers first took control of three small islands just off the east shore of Leyte. By 20 October, designated A-Day, Allied forces had landed on the eastern shore of Leyte and quickly secured the beach front to the point where Gen. MacArthur was able to make an extremely dramatic entrance onto the shores of the invasion. Getting ahold of a portable radio to broadcast this message: "People of the Philippines, I have returned! By the grace of Almighty God, our forces stand again on Philippine soil."

Throughout October, Allied troops swept from the east coast to the west coast battling swamps and Japanese resistance on land while the Imperial Japanese forces planned a major counterattack at sea later known as the Battle of Leyte Gulf: the largest naval battle in the Pacific fought between 23 to 26 October. Japan lost...badly, and Allied forces continued to take control of Leyte, except for Ormoc Bay. Desperate to keep the Philippines to maintain control of oil and rubber supply routes, Japan quickly started moving 34,000 troops on November 11 into Ormoc Bay to provide reinforcements to the forces in Leyte. The

US responded with disruptive measures to prevent resupply and reinforcement measures in a series of land, sea, and air operations.

On land in December 1944, the 77th Infantry Division made a surprise amphibious landing behind enemy lines to help continue the advance. Within the 77th was our next hero, 1st Lt Robert Nett. As a 17-year-old, Nett enlisted in the Connecticut National Guard. Normally, you would need parent consent to enlist at 17. Nett didn't have that so he creased the life out of his birth certificate to make it really hard to read his birth year. It worked and he was in. He later attended and graduated Officer Candidate School and later was assigned a Lieutenant to command Company E, 305th Infantry Regiment, 77th Infantry Division to support the invasion of the Philippines.

Days after the amphibious landing, Nett and his unit came under heavy fire from their main objective: a three story, concrete reinforced blockhouse occupied by Japanese forces which had held off the US advance for two straight days. After ordering 105 mm artillery fire on the blockhouse giving it a modern open space concept, Nett took a hit straight to his neck cutting his jugular vein. Blood squirted out of a needle sized wound but to Nett, this was only flesh wound. He carried on.

Along the path to take out the blockhouse, Nett would crawl to traverse the thick tropical vegetation taking shots at the enemy until he, on several occasions, ran out of ammo leaving him nothing but a bayonet to fight with. Nett would have to resort to hand-to-hand combat on multiple occasions as he moved forward and would kill seven Japanese soldiers en-route, five with his rifle and two others with his bayonet when he ran out of ammo.

Upon reaching close proximity of the enemy position, Nett directed several machine gun teams to alternate between providing cover and advancing. Nett, turned to give a signal to a machine gun crew to move up, and was shot in the right lung as part of his ribcage was blown out of his back. His lung collapsed. Not to worry. Twas only a scratch to that walking force of nature.

Nett continued to supervise the men he led as US forces made their way to the objective and began flushing out the blockhouse with flamethrowers. With the objective complete, Nett's feet were beginning to feel heavy as he pressed on feeling the symptoms of heavy blood loss due to his multiple injuries. He calmly put another Lt. in charge to carry on and Nett walked himself back to receive medical attention to treat his wounds. Nett would later receive the Medal of Honor for his actions, at the age of 22, leading his men in operations to liberate the Philippines.

Interesting Facts

- While in the Philippines, Nett met his wife, an Army Nurse

- Nett continued to serve in both the Korean and Vietnam Wars

- Nett was Considered the "Father of the Officer Candidate School"

- His son also joined Army and rose to the rank of Major

- Nett passed away in 2008

JOHN BASILONE PART 2

By November of 1944, Allied forces were taking back full control of the Philippines islands along with the Mariana islands. The US were closing in as Japan's protective ring of islands was crumbling. The US had their eyes on one of three volcano islands, Iwo Jima, as their next strategic move on the march to Tokyo in what would become the Battle of Iwo Jima in an invasion designated Operation Detachment. Iwo Jima sat almost dead center between Japan and the Mariana Islands.

With two airfields on the Island, Japan used it to launch fighters to intercept Allied raids against Japan, along with offering early warnings to the mainland letting them know well in advance that the enemy was coming. The U.S. wanted it as a strategic location for damaged B-29 bombers to land and to allow P-51 Mustang fighters to escort the bombers during raids on Japan.

Knowing Iwo Jima would be invaded, Japan started preparing for the looming battle in March 1944. Almost a year in advance and well before the loss of the Philippines and Mariana Islands. And prepare they did. The island was defensively fortified with a dense network of bunkers, land mines, camouflaged artillery positions, and 11 miles of tunnels to allow troops to move around the island undetected. Some of their bunkers and underground barracks were anywhere from 75 to 90 ft deep stacked with supplies to hold out for months if needed.

Though a lot of extensive effort had been put into establishing a defensive base in anticipation of an invasion, Japan was not set up to win the battle. They were merely there to slow Allied forces down to give mainland Japan more time to prepare for the coming invasion.

1944 was a year of heavy losses for Japan and the tides had turned for the worse as they had been forced into defensive measures to stop the encroaching forces into their country. War efforts were now focused on protecting Japan so the Japanese forces at Iwo Jima were on their own to defend against 450 American ships, 60,000 Marines, and several thousand Navy Seabees. They didn't stand a chance, but boy did they put up a good fight.

Three days prior to the invasion scheduled for February 19th, 1945, the US started on the offensive with three days of bombardment on the island which the Americans assumed the majority of the Japanese garrison were destroyed by the bomb raids. They were not. The US was unaware of the underground fortress entrenched throughout the island making the results of the bombardment quite limited and the planned invasion a deadly one as this battle would go down as one of the bloodiest fights during the war. War planners in Hawaii thought the battle would last a few days if not a week. They also assumed the beach front would be "easy" to storm and infiltrate.

As the first wave of Marines invaded the Island, they were met with a fifteen-foot steep climb up a black beach of volcanic ash that down shifted a beach storming into a beach walking. Boots sank into the "sand" up to the Marines' knees as they tried to move through it. Luckily, they received no enemy fire after stepping foot on the Island and found the beach undefended. One would quickly assume that the enemy were practically disseminated from the three-day bombardment. Nope. Japanese soldiers were instructed to strategically wait to engage to so the Allied forces would let their guard down before unleashing a massive strike unlike the Pacific theatre had ever seen.

Within an hour of landing, the Imperial Japanese forces would unleash a volume of rattling automatic guns, mortar shells, and exploding mines that would be described as a nightmare in hell. Storming that beach that day, enduring the onslaught of overwhelming firepower from the occupying army was none other than our very own, "Manila John" Basilone.

After his heroic efforts battling wave after wave of Japanese troops defending Guadalcanal, he received the Congressional Medal of Honor and was sent back home a war hero on a war bond tour in 1943. His return was highly publicized as thousands gathered in his hometown for a parade in his honor which made national news. Basilone then toured across the country to help raise funds for the war and quickly achieved a celebrity status of sorts.

The attention and admiration were appreciated but being back home while his brothers in arms continued to fight the war didn't sit well with him. He requested to return to ranks and to continue fighting but was denied. The Corps offered him a commission and a safe assignment stateside, but he refused both. He was reported to have said, "I'm just a plain soldier and want to stay one. I ain't no officer and I ain't no museum piece. I belong back with my outfit." Unhappy, Basilone submitted a second request for reassignment and the Corps finally gave in.

On July 3, 1944, he reenlisted with the Marine Corps. After training in Camp Pendleton, he returned to the Pacific in December of that same year assigned to C Company, 1st Battalion, 27th Marine Regiment, 5th Marine Division. Two months later on February 19, 1945, he was charging the black beaches of Iwo Jima with his men one last time.

Soon after landing on Red Beach II, Basilone and his unit were pinned down by a heavily fortified Japanese blockhouse. And by heavily fortified, I mean practically a concrete block some of which had 10 feet of reinforced concrete walls. Basilone, not one to sit around and do nothing, managed to sneak his way to the blockhouses' flank in the face of a bombardment of heavy fire and sulfur steam. He somehow managed to work his on top of the blockhouse where he did what Basilone did best. Utter obliteration. He single-handedly destroyed the blockhouse stronghold with grenades and demolition certainly living up to his name and reputation.

With the blockhouse out of the way, his fellow Marines were able to advance off the beach front during the early stages of the invasion.

Later on, while attacking Airfield No. 1, a key objective for the American forces, a tank got trapped within an enemy mine field. Under intense mortar and artillery bombardments, Basilone calmly guided the tank to safety during which he was struck by a bursting mortar shell killing our hero instantly at the age of 28.

For his efforts and the ultimate sacrifice for his country, he was awarded posthumously the Navy Cross.

Though war planners originally planned for a week-long battle, Iwo Jima would take over a month as 21,000 determined Japanese forces were dwindled down to roughly 200 at a cost of 26,000 American casualties and almost 7000 dead. Iwo Jima came at a high price tag that would be paid by the lives of men like John Basilone, who in the face of aggressive opposition, fought courageously and daringly to the very end as an inspiration to his comrades and the country he gave it all for.

Interesting Facts

• Basilone married Lena Mae Riggi while training at Camp Pendleton. She died in 1999 at the age of 87 and never remarried.

• The only Marine in WWII to receive both the Medal of Honor and the Navy Cross.

• The iconic image of six Marines raising the flag atop Mount Suribachi was taken on this island.

• Basilone's face is one of four legendary Marines on the Distinguished Marine stamps.

THE CAMOUFLAGE DESIGN FOR THE
U.S. UNIFORMS IN WW2 WAS MADE BY
THE GARDEN EDITOR OF
BETTER HOMES AND GARDEN,
NORVELL GILLESPIE.

HARRY MARTIN

Another hero storming the beach front of Iwo Jima was Harry Martin, a USMC Light Machine Gunner within the 4th Marine Division. He and the men in his unit were part of the first wave to storm the small island on the day the U.S. would see roughly 5,000 casualties. Though this was not the first beach storming Martin would take part in.

Before the Battle of Iwo Jima and after training in Hawaii, he was transported out into the Pacific to charge the shores of the mountainous island of Saipan. It would be there that he'd gain valuable experience against a formidable military force as Allied forces worked for over 3 weeks to take control of the island.

It was on Saipan that he claimed his first samurai sword from a fallen Japanese officer. Where he got the second one is unknown. I can only imagine what it was like trying to get that back on the boat past officers who would claim the sword as "military evidence". From there he was part of a smaller operation to take the island of Tinian.

After additional training, he and his unit stormed the black sand beaches of Iwo Jima on February 19, 1945, the same day as John Basilone, which, as you already know, led to some of the bloodiest battles of the Pacific.

During the initial push to begin the amphibious assault, before Martin and his men could step foot on the sulfuric island as part of the invasion's right flank, the amtrac that was taking them into shore stalled out right in the surf zone. Stuck out in the water, they were literally sitting ducks.

The amtrac operator tried getting her started again as the sitting boat was taking enemy fire from rifles, machine guns, and mortars.

Martin, wanting to get out of a potential tin can coffin, jumped overboard. Soaking wet and weighed down with his gear, someone "gifted" him with a 35 lb machine gun to carry to shore along with everything else he already had with him. Merry Christmas, Martin.

Finally making it to shore, he and a few others set up the machine gun only to look around without a glimpse of the enemy's location. They were all underground, in caves, or bunkers. They couldn't see them first. Often, they discovered where they were after they fired rounds in their direction. Nonetheless, they sent a measly 50 rounds downrange before heavy artillery hit their machine gun and blew it to bits while Martin got hit in the face below his left eye and another gunner got hit in the chest. A Corpsman came over and patched up his face which began to swell up preventing Martin from seeing much at all out of his left eye for several days as he continued to fight on as Allied forces were gaining the advance.

For three days, Martin never saw an enemy force up close as he and his unit moved in the opposite direction of Mount Suribachi. The enemy was so well hidden, Marines would shoot blind at what they thought were potential enemy bunkers or encampments throughout the island. Shooting blind was the norm. It wasn't until a Japanese soldier popped out of a camouflaged entrance into a tunnel that he actually saw one on the third day as the Japanese soldier stormed out to retreat.

As part of the first wave to attack the island and the front of the advance across the island, Martin and his fellow Marines had to make their own playbook to move forward against an enemy that turned out to be much tougher than they ever imagined. Martin would set up his light machine gun and fire rounds into potential enemy locations hoping armor piercing rounds were enough to take out the target. If what they were aiming at was a target at all. If no return fire was received, they led the advance never truly knowing where the enemy was or where they'd pop out.

There were times when Martin found himself in the eerie tunnels as adrenaline rushed through his veins never knowing what he would stumble upon as he made his way further and further underground amid enemy territory.

Suprisingly, even with an injury below his eye that impaired his vision, he managed to survive throughout the 36-day long battle to take the island and was unfortunately shot in the foot on the very last day. Apparently, the Japanese were getting tired of this guy who fought every single day and kicked the Japanese right in the haunches. So, they shot him in the foot on the very last day.

Interesting facts

- Martin tried entering the Marines at the age of 17 by changing his birth certificate birth year from 1925 to 1924… It didn't work.

- Martin didn't see the flag atop Mount Suribachi until the battle was over while he was leaving the island with a bullet wound to the foot.

JACKLYN "JACK" H. LUCAS

A day after Basilone single handedly blew a Japanese blockhouse to smithereens during the Battle of Iwo Jima, another hero, destined for battle, would find himself huddled over not one, but two grenades...and live to talk about it. This marine was Jack Lucas, the youngest marine to receive the military's highest honor at the age of 17, just a few days after his birthday.

And that's where this story gets really interesting. If he was 17 when he went to battle, how old was this kid when he enlisted to begin with? It may be hard to believe but Lucas, at the age 14, lied his way into the military.

As word spread across the globe about Japan's attack on Pearl Harbor, it hit home with 13-year-old Jack Lucas who heard the news over the radio early one Sunday morning at school. While other kids his age at Edwards Military Institute were dealing with puberty, acne, and typical teenage mischief, Lucas wanted nothing more than to go to war against anyone who dared lay a hand on his country.

Not long after, at the age of 14, Lucas ditched school to head to Virginia to enlist. Of course, the military wasn't in the business of sending teenagers to war. Even at 17, you'd have to get your parents' consent. Lucas wasn't even close to 17 so he had to find a way to convince a recruiter that he was. He managed to persuade a notary to swear he was of age in exchange for fifty cents, walked his freakishly developed 5'8", 200-lbs frame into the closest recruiting office, and forged his mother's signature on his enlistment paperwork.

After completing boot camp, he received his long-awaited orders to the front line. Just kidding. He received orders to stay behind at Camp Geiger as an instructor. You think he put in all that work to become a marine at the age of 14 to not fight in battle? Not on his watch. He hid his orders and hopped on the train with the departing party as if he was supposed to be there.

His arrival to California got him one step closer to combat, but that didn't come without obstacles of its own. Showing up with a unit without paperwork certainly doesn't paint the picture that you're where you're supposed to be. However, it was more trouble to send Lucas back than it was to keep him. He got to stay and not long after, Lucas found himself sailing with his battalion toward Pearl Harbor.

Everything was looking promising after arriving in Hawaii until Lucas wrote a letter to his 15-year-old girlfriend that gave away his age. After threatening to leave to join the Army, they let him stay...as a truck driver while his unit shipped out.

Pissed off but not one to give up, Lucas knew that marines that constantly caused trouble got sent to the front lines so that's exactly what he did. He got in fights with sergeants, stole truckloads of beer for his unit, and even beat the living snot out of a military policeman. He spent a lot of time in the brig living off nothing but bread and water. All that effort just to get infuriatingly constipated. Realizing his plan wasn't working along with his bowels, he did what he knew best: go AWOL and figure it out once you get there.

He snuck aboard the USS Deuel and with the help of his cousin who just so happened to be on board, hid for 29 days eating scraps and practically breadcrumbs to survive, doing his best not to get caught in hope he wouldn't get sent back to Hawaii. Just days before he would be placed on the " deserter list", he turned himself in to an officer on board. His punishment? He was assigned as a rifleman within C Company, 1st Battalion, 26th Marines, 5th Division heading to combat. He got exactly what he wanted, and just days before storming the beaches of Iwo Jima, he turned 17.

On February 19, he stormed the beaches with the first few waves of marines to land on shore. Bullets were flying everywhere, mortal fire was all around, dust from volcanic ash was in the air, and people were being blown apart, but the chaos didn't deter Lucas one bit. This is exactly where he wanted to be.

The next day, Lucas and three other marines were making their way toward the Japanese airstrip when they came upon an enemy pillbox. They quickly took cover within one of two parallel trenches that were dug by the Japanese, when 11 enemy soldiers made their way through tunnels in the other trench only six feet away. With no time to aim, the marines fired away as Lucas landed a headshot before his rifle jammed.

Looking down at his weapon, he noticed two grenades directly in front of his fellow marines. Yelling, " Grenade!" Lucas superman leaped over the first using his rifle to shove it deep into the volcanic sand and reached out with his arm to grab the other covering them both with his body.

The explosion of first grenade sent him into the air before he landed on his back still holding the second grenade, which didn't explode. The other three marines, thinking he was dead, carried on the fight and left him. Only, he wasn't dead and was every bit conscious throughout the whole thing though barely breathing.The grenade sent over 200 pieces of shrapnel into his body some of which punctured his lung. It was all he could do to wave with his left hand to get help, as his mouth kept filling up with blood.

Another marine from a different unit found him and called over a Corpsman who began working on him with a dose of morphine when a Japanese soldier popped out of a hole, but the Corpsman, who didn't typically carry weapons, shot him unloading 18 rounds into him saving both of their lives.

After surviving a round of mortal fire, he was put onto a stretcher to head back to the shore but not without a stretcher-bearer stumbling and dropping his end causing Lucas to split his head open on a rock. Thank goodness for morphine. Lucas waited on shore until nightfall before being transported to ship when a wave about took Lucas with it, but he was luckily caught by the foot and pulled back into the boat.

After 20 plus operations, Lucas managed to survive as he returned to the US a celebrated hero. He received the Medal of Honor on October 5, 1945 from President Truman.

Interesting facts

• Years after the war, he joined the Army in 1961 in the 82nd Airborne Division as a paratrooper. During a training jump, both parachutes malfunctioned, but he somehow survived. Of course, if you can survive a grenade...what's a 3,500 foot freefall to the ground? Just an ordinary Tuesday for Lucas.

• Lucas died in 2008 in the same city this book was written: Hattiesburg, Mississippi.

FROM THE BEGINNING OF THE WAR TO THE END, THE U.S. DEFENSE BUDGET INCREASED

MORE THAN 30-FOLD

FROM

$1.9B TO $59.8B.

HERSHEL "WOODY" WILLIAMS

On February 21, 1945, Corporal Hershel "Woody" Williams landed on the beaches of Iwo Jima a day after Jack Lucas was sent into the air protecting his fellow marines from two grenades. Two days later, on February 23rd, Williams would continuously put himself in harm's way as he cleared out the enemy pillbox after pillbox with nothing but a flamethrower. Though survival wasn't anything new to him.

Williams was born premature in 1923 the youngest of 11 children on a farm. He came in a light weight at a whopping 3.5 pounds and wasn't expected to live. Somehow managing to survive his birth, he would go on to face more hardships: losing his father to a heart attack and several siblings to a flu pandemic. He had seen his fair share of struggles as he grew up.

Fast forward to 1942, Williams tried to enlist with Marines Corps but was denied...because of his height. At 5'6", the Marines deemed him too short to ride this ride. Luckily in 1943, the military changed their height restriction giving Williams a second chance.

During training, he and a few others were handed flamethrowers with zero instructions on how to use them or what fuel to use. They had to figure it out on their own. They tried kerosene, gasoline, and diesel with abysmal results. It wasn't until a gunnery sergeant showed up with a barrel of jet fuel mixed with diesel that they had something worth taking into combat. With the mystery concoction in the tank, these men could blast out an inferno at 3,500 degrees F.

After training to be a demolition man and in the art of wielding flamethrowers, he was sent to the Pacific to fight in the Battle of Guam which involved a lot of creeping and crawling through thick, tropical jungle terrain. He remained stationed at Guam until February 1945 when he and the rest of the 3rd Marine division were told they were shipping out for battle though he had no idea where.

He was assigned to Company C, 1st Battalion, 21st Marine Regiment, 3rd Marine Division to take Iwo Jima as a reserve unit. He and most of the men aboard had never heard of the place. During transit, they were briefed that Iwo Jima was a small island, 2 miles wide and 5 miles long and the battle would last only a few days, a week at the latest and that they, a reserve unit, would most likely never get off the ship. Little did they know the invasion of Iwo Jima would take over a month and at a significant cost of life and soon enough, just two days after the initial invasion, William's unit was called into battle.

Unlike the battles in Guam, Iwo Jima looked completely wiped out. It was no tropical paradise. In Guam, you could hide among the vegetation. At Iwo Jima, there was hardly anywhere to take cover. The few places to hide were within a crater created by the explosion of mortars and heavy artillery or you had to dig your own within the black, volcanic sand.

Williams described digging into the sand as digging into marbles. You could try to dig a hole, but the surrounding sand would immediately fill in the hole. Running on it was nearly impossible. Boots sank knee deep with each step which made swift movements a challenge they had not seen or experienced before.

And with next to zero protection from the sun, the place was hot as hell. Williams, described the miserable heat, " You could take a C-ration can of food and dig a hole and bury it, and the next morning, you could have hot food." But only if you remembered where you buried it amidst the chaos during the battle.

Four days after the initial beach invasion, Williams's unit, with few places to take cover to push the advance, was trying without success to make a path through a network of steel reinforced pillboxes, aka bunkers. It would seem these Marines would have to push through what felt like an impossible wall of resistance. The Japanese, with concrete protected bunkers and miles of underground tunnels to maneuver, had the upper hand as they fought from a protected area while the marines struggled immensely to fight out in the open trying their best to move from crater to crater. Some Japanese were hidden inside 50-gallon barrels buried in the sand. They'd crack the lid just enough to fire out of and close the lid as they blinded into the terrain once again.

Completely pinned down by heavy enemy fire, the company commander called a meeting inside a crater to come up with a plan. He asked Williams, the only demolition sergeant left, if he could try and take the pillboxes with his flamethrower. Williams said he'd try since nothing else was working.

With four Marine riflemen providing cover fire, it was Williams' job to encroach on the enemy pillbox and take it out. With his four men providing crossfire, he crawled with his heavy, 65 lb fuel tank strapped to his back to get within close enough range of the bunker. During his one man advance, he could hear bullets pinging off his tank as Japanese soldiers tried taking him out. One solid hit and he'd go up in flames.

Within the effective range of 65 feet, he aimed and pulled the trigger as dragon breath consumed the pillbox and the occupants with it. To the unit's surprise, the method worked. Williams continued this approach for hours going from one pillbox to the next. If he ran out of fuel which only lasted about 72 seconds at full blast, he'd run back to his unit, pick up another flamethrower and run right back to the next pillbox.

On one occasion that day, Williams tried to approach the pillbox from the front but was under too much fire to get within effective range. He decided to go around taking the pillbox from the flank. As he got close to the pillbox and saw smoke coming out from a vent. The Japanese's ammunition gave off a lot of smoke when fired. This smoke was coming out of the air vent giving Williams an easy entry point to fire his flamethrower into the pillbox. He stuck the nozzle of his flamethrower down in the vent and before he could pull the trigger, 4 or 5 came rushing out with weapons and bayonets to take Williams out. Heavily outnumbered, Williams gave a quick spray of flames and took them out before they could get to him.

Williams was able to take out seven pillboxes using six different flamethrowers that day in efforts to capture the island which enabled the advance once they were taken out. Somehow, he managed to accomplish his mission without as much as a scratch. Unfortunately, the Marines providing the cover fire were not so fortunately. Two of the four lost their lives protecting Williams during the advance. He would later receive the medal of honor for his effort in the advance on Iwo Jima.

Interesting Facts

· Williams chose the Marines over the Army because he liked the way the Marines looked in their uniforms versus the Army which he considered ugly.

· On the same day of his heroic efforts, Williams standing just 1000 yards away from Mount Suribachi, witnessed the historical raising of the flag by a small crew of fellow Marines.

· Of the 13 Marines who received the Medal of Honor, Williams is the only one still living as of the publishing of this book.

· Williams, while filling out paperwork to enlist, forgot to fill in a section under "Religion". Having never been to church, he peeked at the paperwork of a kid next to him who put a "C" under that section. Williams did the same. At boot camp, Williams was sent to attend Mass since he identified on his paperwork as a Catholic.

HARRY L. MARTIN

During the early hours on the last day of the Battle of Iwo Jima on March 26, 1945, things were settling down for the Allied forces on the volcanic island. The Japanese had pretty much been defeated as the fire fights were becoming less frequent. Most troops were getting ready to depart the island for good the very next day especially the Marines within the 5th Marine Division who had been there since the invasion on February 19th. The 5th, compared to the 3rd and 4th Marine Divisions on the island, had seen the most casualties.

Men were trading foxholes for tents near the shore as a small tent city had been constructed for officers and enlisted alike. Major fire fights with the enemy on the island seemed all but distant though U.S. troops would quickly find out that was far from the case.

At 0400, a surprise attack began that the men involved who had their sights on leaving the island would never forget. The Japanese commander, Lt. Gen. Tadamichi Kuribayashi, issued an order to what was left of his men, roughly 300 to 600 troops, as one final attack against the western beach at the base of Mount Suribachi. What made matters worse, the Japanese attacked as one Marine battalion was leaving and before an Army Infantry Regiment could arrive. The perfect storm would allow them easy access to infiltrate into the tent city while many occupants were fast asleep.

The attack began with heavy artillery hitting the command tent followed by a unit of Japanese soldiers marching in Marine uniforms stolen from fallen Marines. English-speaking officers shouting marching commands just as the marines would give way to an opportunity to literally march their way toward the tent city before being detected.

Hundreds of Japanese soldiers rushed into camps slicing through tents and throwing in grenades followed by emptying their weapons into the startled occupants. Japanese officers wielding samurai swords seemed to be everywhere slicing through tents and attacking those inside. Six were killed and 19 wounded before most could wipe the sleep from their eyes.

Confusion and panic spread thick as the Japanese had overrun several units almost effortlessly as they began to occupy trenches, foxholes, and even pillboxes they had lost earlier in the battle. This was no banzai attack. This was a well-planned attempt to cause mass confusion and high casualties.

The line of defense was held mainly from the efforts of 1st Lt. Harry Martin and his men within Company C, Fifth Pioneer Battalion, Fifth Marine Division. Not to be confused with the other Harry Martin on the island who, on the very same day, got shot in the foot.

The 5th Pioneer Battalion was composed of African American Marines commanded by white officers and sadly, underappreciated for their efforts and sacrifices during the battle of Iwo Jima (and the war at large). Though they went through the same rigorous training, some didn't receive infantry training (along with racial discrimination on top of it), the African American Marines were more often used to unload supplies and run ammunition to Marines fighting on the front lines and bring the fallen back with them.

On this day, after the Japanese had attacked through several units, the African American Marines were ready to prove their worth in battle. Ivan Prall, an NCO on the island as a switchboard operator recalled the response of the men within the 5th Pioneer Battalion that day as, "Extraordinary."

Martin, as platoon leader of the 5th Pioneer Battalion, formed a line with the men around him and held off the initial attack. After holding off the first wave, his next move was to save some of his wounded men that were surrounded by enemy troops. Risking his own life and getting wounded twice in the process, he killed any Japanese soldier who tried to stop him as he made his way to his men and got them back behind friendly lines.

When four Japanese troops took control of an abandoned machine gun pit, Martin, carrying nothing but his pistol, charged after and killed all four occupants. Realizing that his men could not withstand another organized assault, Martin led the charge straight into the enemy force permanently disrupting and disorganizing them before being mortally wounded by a grenade at the age of 34.

Because of Martin's efforts and that of the men he led, he successfully allowed U.S. forces to reorganize and counterattack against the hostile forces successfully securing the island at 0900 that morning, just a few hours after Martin's death. Martin was posthumously awarded the Medal of Honor.

Interesting Facts

- There are very few photos taken of African American Marines at Iwo Jima though they were present and vitally important.

- Martin was the last Marine awarded the Medal of Honor in the battle of Iwo Jima.

- Martin was originally buried in the 5th Division Cemetery at Iwo Jima before his remains were returned to Ohio in 1948 at the request of his mother.

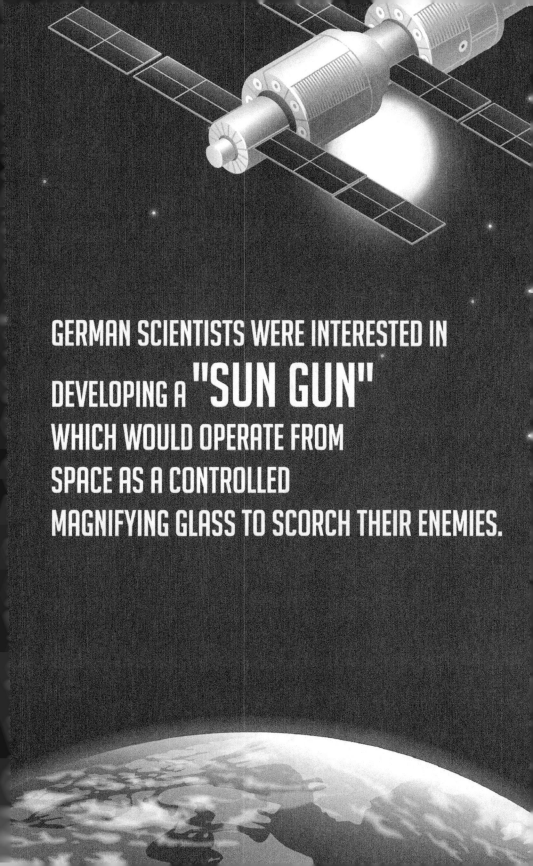

DAVID M. GONZALES

On April 25, 1945, it was a hot and humid day as the 32nd Infantry Division of the US Army was making their way along the Villa Verde Trail: a 27-mile dirt and muddy path among dense vegetation on Luzon, the largest island in the Philippines.

A few years back in 1941, the Japanese had invaded the island and captured it kicking our American butts out of it. It was considered a critical strategic location during the war in the Pacific Theatre. It wasn't until January 1945 that the US and Philippine troops launched an attack to take back the island. 70 Allied warships and an estimated 175,000 troops landed on the island to support the effort.

From 1941 to 1945, Japanese forces had developed an intricate network of caves and tunnels to hide and move around the island undetected. The enemy was highly camouflaged among the rough terrain, advancing across the island was slow and dangerous. To counter, The US Army Air Corps used 500-pound bombs with delayed fuses. These heavy bombs of explosive freedom would bury themselves deep into the ground before exploding, collapsing all underground infrastructure nearby. They were incredibly effective...if they hit the right target.

Within a few months of invading the Philippines, the US had captured all key parts of the islands though some enemy forces were still hunkered down in the mountains with access to supplies and reinforcements. Which is why the 32nd was assigned to securing the Villa Verde Trail to disrupt Japanese supply lines.

Pfc. David M. Gonzales, a Mexican American aged 21, was among the infantry in that division securing the route. Gonzales grew up the oldest of 14 children of Mexican immigrants in Pacoima, California. Soon after getting married, he enlisted in the Army and shipped overseas after only a brief visit home to say goodbye to his wife and newborn son. His final words to his wife, " Take good care of my son. I won't be coming home."

The route to disrupt supply lines made it impossible for large support vehicles to accompany the troops so the soldiers set off on foot to complete the mission. As they made their way, they encountered and were pinned down by Japanese forces on what was designated hill 507. US planes dropped one large 500-pound delayed detonation bomb to destroy Japanese hiding places. Unfortunately, one of those bombs landed on the wrong hill near Gonzales' unit. The explosion buried and trapped five American soldiers in their standing foxholes.

Without hesitation, Gonzalez grabbed an entrenching shovel and crawled 15 yards amid heavy machine gun fire to dig out his comrades. His commanding officer also crawled over and was beginning to dig before being hit by enemy fire and was killed in his efforts. Without stopping, Gonzalez used his shovel and hands to free the first man trapped while still under a hail of fire. Putting himself and further harm's way, he stood up to be in a better vantage point to dig faster to save a second and third soldier. As the third man was freed, Gonzales was hit and killed.

All five who were trapped were eventually rescued and made it to safety. The third man rescued was Sgt. William W. Kouts who would later write the report describing Gonzales' heroic effort resulting in him being awarded the Medal of Honor posthumously by President Harry Truman on December 8, 1954.

Interesting Facts

• At a ceremony, David Gonzales Jr. noticed the photo they had on record for his father was of someone else. The photo of a soldier had been erroneously displayed in the Pentagon's Hall of Heroes for years.

• Gonzales was originally buried in the Philippines in 1945, but his remains were shipped back to the US in 1949 and he was laid to rest in Los Angeles, California.

• Gonzales's half-brother, Phillip M. Duarte, also joined the military and was killed in action in Korea. They are buried side by side.

CHAPTER 3:
EUROPEAN THEATRE
HEROES

"Battle is the most magnificent competition
in which a human being can indulge.
It brings out all that is best;
it removes all that is base.
All men are afraid in battle.
The coward is the one who
lets his fear overcome his sense of duty.
Duty is the essence of manhood."
~ George S. Patton

VAN T. BARFOOT

In January of 1944, L Company, 157th Infantry, 45th Infantry Division landed in Anzio, Italy in the campaign to push Germany out of Italy. Within this division was a 24-year-old Technical Sergeant Van Barfoot, a farm raised Mississippi resident, who had already been awarded a Bronze and Silver Star for his efforts during the invasion of Sicily in July 1943 and the invasion of mainland Italy in December of that same year. From January through May of 1944, his unit had made it to Carano, Italy and had been heavily engaged in an assault against German forces for weeks.

Day in and day out, Allied forces tried everything they could to bust through the German stronghold, literally littered with mine fields, without much luck at all. Over the weeks, Barfoot, while on day and night patrols, familiarized himself with the lay of the battlefield along with the interfering minefields that were, among other things, making it extremely dangerous to advance.

On May 23, Barfoot requested to lead his squad through the enemy's territory at their flank with minimal casualties. With approval of his superiors, he led his men through the minefield near their location. Barfoot then placed his men in a position to defend a potential withdrawal and risked his own life and proceeding along. He crawled up to the first machine gun on the far-right flank of the German defense and blew it up with a grenade killing two and injuring three others. And the fun was just getting started along with Barfoot's lethal reputation among the German forces close by.

He continued along their defensive line to the closest gun emplacement and used his submachine gun to kill two more along with injuring and capturing three others. I can only imagine word was spreading over German communications of a one-man army taking out their encampments one by one like some sort of trench spartan. By the time he made it to the third emplacement, the Germans dropped their weapons and surrendered to him. Hope was all lost.

Barfoot, not having time to babysit German prisoners, continued leaving them behind to be handled by his support squad while he captured more enemy forces totaling seventeen by the end. But Barfoot's day was not done.

He and his men were occupying that territory when later that afternoon, the Germans launched a fierce counterattack against Barfoot and his men by bringing to the fight three tanks to take him out. I'm sure they felt pretty confident going in sensing the opposition was merely a few men with flesh for armor. They should have brought ten. This was Barfoot we're talking about.

With a bazooka in hand, he ordered his men to take cover in the ditch while he took the offensive. Within 75 yards, he shot and nailed the lead tank, disabling it and the enemy advancement. The other two tanks, now seeing firsthand the work of the trench spartan ditched their plan and headed in different directions. The crew within the disabled tank tried to evacuate but they were destroyed by Barfoot who had sprinted the 75-yard distance to take them out with his submachine gun.

Barfoot continued into enemy territory because why stop at that point? He soon located two recently abandoned German artillery pieces and disabled one of them by placing a demolition charge within the breech.

On the route back to his platoon, and even though he was exhausted from being awesome, he managed to help two of his seriously wounded men travel 1700 yards back to safety.

We're talking a mile here people. This dude was relentless.

He was later awarded the Medal of Honor and had the option to return home to receive the award or stay in the field. Like a boss, he chose to be awarded in the field to stay in the fight with his men. Barfoot would go on to live a long life, retiring as a Colonel after over 30 years of service, and passing away at the age of 92 in 2012.

Interesting Facts

- Barfoot was quarter Choctaw

- He served in 3 wars: WWII, Korea, and Vietnam.

- One of the biggest battles he fought later in life was with the local homeowner's association which would not allow him to keep his flagpole in his front yard. The news caught word of it and the HOA was figuratively obliterated just like that tank back in Italy.

- TSgt Barfoot was battlefield commissioned to Second Lieutenant for his efforts in battle.

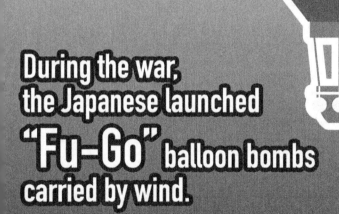

During the war,
the Japanese launched
"Fu-Go" balloon bombs
carried by wind.

Some of which reached
as far as Michigan
but the tactic was very ineffective.

CHARLES H. COOLIDGE

One month after Allied forces captured Rome, the 36th Infantry Division was pulled from Italy in August 1944 to support the effort to invade southern France known as Operation Avalanche. From southern France, the 36th division stayed on the front line pushing their way closer and closer to the German border as they met resistance not only from German troops but also from the harsh winter looming as summer fell into fall.

Within the division was TSgt Charles Coolidge and his twelve-man squad moving eastward with the objective of taking Hill 623, near Belmont sur Buttant, France. A mere 50 miles from the German border.

On October 24, 1944, Coolidge and his men took the hill with zero resistance. With no officers with his squad to call orders, Coolidge radioed back to his superiors telling them they'd taken the objective and were awaiting further orders. Their new orders: hold the hill and dig in.

Soon after, he found a German platoon within the woods on the hill. Taking one of his men with him, George Ferguson, who could speak just enough German to get in trouble, he met with the Germans. The balls of this guy. Meeting out in the open with the enemy as if they were about to simply flip a coin at the start of a game to see who gets the ball first. But this was simply Coolidge's style.

After some chit chat, he asked Ferguson to ask the Germans if they wanted to give up. Before they could surrender, Coolidge noticed a German soldier drawing a weapon to shoot Ferguson. Coolidge quickly shot the German and another before a firefight broke out that would last four days. With no officer around, Coolidge, aged 23, immediately took command and led his men, most of whom had never seen combat, to repulse every assault Germany could throw at them.

Outnumbered, Coolidge continued to contact his command for support, but support never came. Even still, they held off every assault and on the fourth day of fighting, the Germans brought up tanks to take them out.

One tank leading the rest stopped within 25 - 35 yards of Coolidge's position. The tank commander opened the hatch and poked his upper body outside. Coolidge, balls of steel, stood up and looked him dead in the eyes. The German, in perfect English, asked, "Do you guys want to give up? " The very same question Coolidge asked Ferguson to ask the Germans just four days before. Coolidge calmly responded, " I'm sorry, Mac. You've got to come and get me. " The tank commander tucked back into the tank and closed the hatch before turning the tank's barrel at Coolidge point blank and fired...and missed.

And missed, and missed, and missed, and missed again. The tank shot at him five times at close range and as Coolidge took cover behind trees and ran in the opposite direction of the barrel. The tank stopped firing after the fifth unsuccessful shot, not wanting to waste any more precious ammo on a U.S. soldier that just would not seem to die.

Coolidge needed something to take out the tank and found a bazooka. Imagine his luck and excitement as he picked it up and charged 10 yards closer, dropped to his knee to aim, and fired...but nothing happened. The bazooka wouldn't fire. The battery needed to ignite the powder charge in the rocket was missing. Rats. He ditched the bazooka and started throwing grenades. He then went from one of his soldiers to the next yelling and ordering them to throw as many grenades as they could.

Even after holding the hill for four days, Coolidge recognized they could no longer withstand the overwhelming German force and ordered a withdrawal off the hill with him being the last one to leave to ensure a safe escape for his men. He and his squad were credited with killing 26 enemy soldiers and wounding over 60 while defending the hill. He later received the Medal of Honor for his courage and leadership during those four days.

Interesting Facts

- The soldiers within the 36th Infantry Division were known as the T-Patchers, a nickname given from the insignia worn by the soldiers of an olive drab "T" on a light blue arrowhead.

- Coolidge's son, Charles H. Coolidge Jr., also joined the military and rose to the rank of Lt. Gen. in the U.S. Air Force.

- Coolidge was one of 12 portraits of Medal of Honor recipients on the Medal of Honor stamps.

BERNARD P. BELL

In December of 1944, six months after D-Day, Allied forces had pushed all but a few pockets of German forces out of France. To finish the job, Company I, 142nd Infantry Regiment, 36th Infantry Division took on German forces in Selestat, France, close to the border of Germany.

On 5 December 1944, Germans had bunkered down in a well-fortified building sending buckets of bullets 100 yards away toward American forces to prevent their advance. TSgt John Bell, feeling froggy, ordered his men to cover him as he dashed across a football field's stretch of hazardous territory. Bullets whizzed by as he approached the building just before kicking the door wide open with the power of adrenaline-fueled democracy.

As the door slammed open, he opened fire and began shouting to the occupants to surrender. The Germans must have thought the maniac at their door was more beast than human because all ten of them dropped their weapons and filed out of the building to surrender.

Bell, not done yet, continued the offensive toward a large factory and single handedly eliminated an enemy position within the vicinity.

Once the platoon caught up to seize the entire factory, they were able to capture 85 enemy troops while the remainder retreated. For his efforts that day, he received the Distinguished Service Cross though this story doesn't end there.

From Selestat he and his unit headed down south just fifteen miles to the small town of 700 people called Mittelwihr, France, to continue the advance. It was there that TSgt Bernard Bell and his eight man squad would be heavily outnumbered but not outgunned in a battle over a schoolhouse of all places. Get ready for this one because class is officially in session.

On the morning of December 18, 1944, German troops were occupying said schoolhouse and Bell was concerned they weren't quite getting a quality education on American military dominance. Taking it upon himself to ensure they received an academic lesson of the highest semi-automatic caliber, he decided he and his 8 men would take control of the school once and for all.

113

At the entrance, two German troops stood watch on the early morning shift. As they were standing there freezing their butts off talking trash about the other troops hanging out inside where it was warm, an American soldier came out of nowhere and scared the loving life out of them. They surrendered without that one-man army ever firing his weapon. It was Bell again doing what he did best.

Moments before he ninja'd his way over to them, he pulled a move straight out of his own playbook ordering his men to cover him as he made his way to the building.

After taking them prisoner, Bell entered the schoolhouse and found twenty-six others hiding out in the cellar. I'm sure they were surprised and pissed when they found out that a single American soldier had invaded their hideout and the two guards, who had one job, failed.

Twenty-six versus one is a tough challenge for anyone... except for Bell. Without an escape route, Bell threatened to teach them a lesson of what happens to a gaggle of soldiers in a room with live grenades.

I don't know if Bell spoke German or if the Germans spoke English. What I do know is that grenades are an international language understood by all sides. They surrendered.

From there, Bell and his men occupied the schoolhouse and prepared for a counterattack from enemy forces which showed up the next day. A quality education is hard to come by and the Germans wanted a piece of it.

German forces bombarded the schoolhouse with artillery and mortar rounds which constantly disrupted communications with the company commander. Bell repeatedly put himself in harm's way to repair comm lines to keep his superior officer informed of how the lecture was going with his new batch of international students. His students were hardheaded but Bell was more than determined to deliver the message.

Throughout the day, Bell and his men would fire German firearms in hopes that unsuspecting forces would believe friendly forces had infiltrated the schoolhouse. Like flies to a light, it worked like a charm as the Americans took more prisoners or took them out as they approached the building. Poor suckers.

The next day, a German tank showed up and shot round after round of heavy artillery, almost destroying the upper floors. Bell, undeterred by the destruction, climbed over rubble to the second floor as he and his men directed fire at the tank forcing it to retreat.

After taking out several more foot soldiers with mortar fire, he called in some armored support of his own. Once a friendly tank arrived, he stood exposed to small-arms fire just outside the tank to tell the occupants where to fire. He pointed out walls the Germans were using to encroach on the building. As the tank obliterated the hostile forces defenses, Bell directed machine gun fire on the enemy to mow them down.

Thanks to his courage and bravery, Bell and his men were able to keep 150 opposing troops at bay, killing eighty-seven and capturing forty-two. He personally killed more than twenty and captured thirty-three delivering an education of the highest degree. I'm sure the German class of '44 would never forget their time with Professor Bell.

Class dismissed.

Interesting Facts

- Bell was one of 10 Medal of Honor recipients from West Virginia during WW2. One of those 10 was also a hero you have already read about: Hershel "Woody" Williams.

WILLIAM HITLER

HITLER'S NEPHEW,

SERVED IN THE U.S. NAVY DURING THE WAR.

JOHN R. FOX

Before the invasion into Europe, and even before the completion of the North African Campaign, the U.S. and the British could not agree as to which route to invade Europe to best whoop some German tail. The U.S. wanted the most direct route by invading France. The British wanted to go through Italy. So how did they settle it? They chose to do both.

A smaller Allied force would invade Sicily on July 10, 1943 while a larger Allied force would invade France much later in the summer of 1944. A world war compromise in the making where no one left truly happy, but everyone was glad to stop arguing about it.

After the successful invasion of Sicily at the toe end of the boot shaped country, Allied forces made their way to continental Italy and up through several defensive lines before finally pushing Axis forces up to the very top at the Gothic Line.

The Gothic Line was the last major defensive line along the summits of the Apennine Mountains in northern Italy. This bad boy was stacked with over 2,000 machine gun nests, bunkers, artillery fighting positions, observation posts, and an awful terrain that made breaching the line exceedingly difficult.

After making steady gains from the latter half of 1943 and the first half of 1944, a large chunk of Allied forces were relocated to support the invasion of France during Operation Overlord. That didn't leave much to finish off the Italian campaign so to support the effort, the 92nd

Infantry Division were sent to Italy.

What was uncommon about the 92nd Infantry Division, nicknamed the Buffalo Soldiers, was that it was a segregated African American Division and the only African American infantry division to see combat during WW2.

From their landing in Naples Italy in August 1944 to the end of that same year, the Buffalo Soldiers continued to push Axis forces northward into the hilly terrain occupying the small village of Sommocolonia, Italy by December which was a part of the Gothic Line.

Sommocolonia is a hilltop village, old as dirt but a beautiful landscape. Most construction was built during the Middle Ages and Renaissance eras. And this place was old school, like communicating with other local villages via smoke signals.

Because of the harsh terrain, the military had a really hard time getting supplies to units like the 92nd so they purchased horses and donkeys along the way which is how most supplies made it up to the very top to Sommocolonia. Thank goodness they did because the Sommocolonians were living off chestnuts just to survive. The African American soldiers within the 92nd shared their field rations with them to get them through the bitter winter.

Among the men within the 92nd was 1st Lt John Fox, a forward observer for his unit.

Earlier that year in September, Allied forces were able to pierce the Gothic Line reaching Rimini, Italy. To help relieve pressure at Rimini, the Axis force planned the Battle of Garfagnana known as Operation Winter Storm. Garfagnana was a small area of the Gothic Line and the objective was to conquer several small towns including Sommocolonia to successfully push the Allies back roughly 16 miles.

On Christmas, the beginning stages of Operation Winter Storm were taking place at Sommocolonia as Axis forces dressed in civilian clothing started occupying the village forcing most of the infantry troops to withdraw. Fox and some members of his party volunteered to remain behind in order to direct defensive artillery fire to slow the enemy's advance.

By 0400 on December 26th, hostile forces had control of most of the village and were attacking in force. Fox and members of his party were positioned on the second floor of a building calling coordinates for artillery fire from 75 heavy artillery guns. Even with the amount of defensive fire, German troops continued to advance. Fox and his small observer party were heavily outnumbered.

With each artillery strike called in by Fox, the coordinates continued to get closer and closer to his position. His final call, he ordered all 75 guns to train their fire on his location. Thinking it was a mistake, the soldier who received the message was stunned knowing if he fired, Fox would have slim chances of surviving. After the soldier called in his concerns, Fox responded, " Fire it! There's more of them than there are of us. Give them hell!" And hell was given as heavy artillery rained down from above on his position delaying advance.

The delay in the Axis advance gave the Allied forces precious time to reorganize and retake Sommocolonia by January 1, 1945. As Allied forces re-entered the village, they found Fox's body along with the 8 Italian soldiers with him amid 100 German bodies. Lt Fox would later receive the Medal of Honor posthumously but not for many decades. On January 12, 1997, Fox, along with 6 other African Americans who fought in WW2, would receive the U.S. Military's highest honor.

Interesting Facts

• Fox has his own G.I. Joe action figure.

• He participated in the Army ROTC under the leadership of Capt. Aaron R. Fisher, a WW1 veteran

• As of 2018, the village population of Sommocolonia was a whopping 22 people.

VITO R. BERTOLDO

During the worst winter Europe had seen in 20 years, Germany was losing steam during the Battle of the Bulge. Months prior, Hitler held a meeting with his top brass of the SS, who he trusted, to lay out his plan to infiltrate the Allied defensive line with a surprise counter-offensive. This was in September just a few months after his top leadership of the traditional standing army of Germany (among others) tried to assassinate the Third Reich.

His plan, a concentrated effort to penetrate the US and British forces, separate the two military powers meanwhile encircling them to their utter destruction and cut off their supply point at the port of Antwerp in four days.

Sounds promising until you realize that Germany would have to practically Blitzkrieg their way through roughly 150 miles worth of bloody battle...

In. Four. Days.

The front lines had been stagnant for months, Germany had been slowly losing ground, and this was his plan to turn the tide of war. His hope was to bring the Allied powers to the negotiation table for a peace treaty in hopes to give him more time to prepare for the encroaching attacks from the Soviet Union from the east.

As you can imagine his top military leadership objected to the idea and proposed an alternative that didn't lead to utter devastation. Hitler's response, " Oh, I see your point. I, am a rational and logical human being, and see the value in your alternate as opposed to my own and will reconsider my plans." Just kidding. He said, " Nein!!" in a nutshell.

They went through with the plan which started on December 16, 1944 and... they didn't reach the port. They really didn't get very far at all, but boy did they put up a fight which I guess isn't too difficult when troops are jacked up on meth.

The " Bulge" would go down in history as the bloodiest single battle by the US in WW2 and the third deadliest in US history.

123

As German efforts during the surprise attack were on the brink of failure, Hitler scheduled another meeting with his generals for his next plan to attack farther down south. His plan? Penetrate a weak point in the US Third Army, which was being directed up north to deal with the Battle of the Bulge. After invading the line, they would push their way to Strasbourg, France in an operation known as Operation Northwind. From there, Operation Dentist would kick into place to attack the US Third Army from the rear to destroy them like Nazi flouride to a cavity from the gradual build-up of freedom infused plaque. This would hopefully relieve pressure up north where the Germans were losing ground in the Ardennes Forest.

On December 28, 1944, the day of the meeting, Hitler told his division commanders, "This attack has a very clear objective, namely the destruction of the enemy forces. There is not a matter of prestige involved here. It is a matter of destroying and exterminating the enemy forces wherever we find them."

The attack started on December 31, 1944 and would become the last major assault by Germany on the Western front during the war. On the way to Strasbourg is the small village of Hatten which would find itself in the heart of battle.

Located there was the command post (CP) for the 1st Battalion, 242nd Infantry Regiment. To prepare for the looming attack by Germany, the battalion issued an order that each company would supply a detail of three men to serve as the battalion command post guard. In the three that came from the 42nd Infantry Division was our very unlikely hero: Vito R. Bertoldo.

Bertoldo was a shy and lanky 25-year-old working as coal miner and truck driver before joining the army. Originally, he was exempt from the draft due to hot garbage eyesight and was only approved for limited duty serving as a military policeman. After the invasion of Europe and in desperate need of replacements, the Army relooked at their supply of limited duty men and Bertoldo managed to talk his way into an infantry assignment.

That assignment probably sounded pretty cool as he trained for the front line only to be assigned to the 42nd …. as a cook.

So how did Pfc Bertoldo get his chance as combat assigned to the three-man detail to defend the CP? Was it because he made a mean bowl of soup? Nope. Was it because his company commander, Capt. Willaim Corson, saw an innate combat ability within Bertoldo? Nope. It was because Capt. Corson could not stand his guts.

Corson had one disciplinary problem and that was Bertoldo. This cook just couldn't get along with the mess sergeant so when the request came down from the battalion, Capt. Corson put Bertoldo at the top of the list. Good riddance he thought.

On January 9, 1945, while Bertoldo was standing guard of the CP entrance during a bone cold winter's day, German forces started decorating the town in bullets. The battalion staff withdrew as Bertoldo and two other infantrymen defended the line. A group of German soldiers arrived and faked a surrender, killing the other two men in Bertoldo's detail leaving him heavily outnumbered and outgunned.

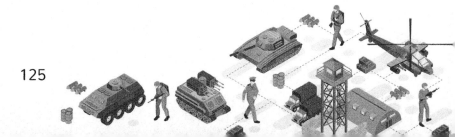

Bertoldo could have retreated at that point but decided to stay and hold the line. Bertoldo left his place of defense and manned a machine gun out in the open in the middle of the street for almost 12 hours. Why stand out in the open? Absolutely no idea. Maybe his defenseless position gave hostile troops the warm fuzzies that he wasn't much of a threat as they made their approach.

Where most soldiers were fighting building to building playing a lethal game hide and seek, Bertoldo was that one kid in the neighborhood who seemed to not understand the rules of the game. Regardless of the reason, he was still able to drive back attacks completely exposed to small-arms fire and 88-mm artillery, which fired ammunition about the length of a man's leg, which would absolutely blow you to shreds.

He eventually repositioned inside the CP firing his machine gun through a window after strapping it to a table. He defended the main approach to the building even as tanks 75 yards away pointed 88-mm artillery in his direction used for taking out tanks and aircrafts. One direct hit and Bertoldo's Army issued flesh armor wouldn't cut it. One shell went straight into the CP while the explosion blasted Bertoldo across the room. Even with his ears plagued with a high-pitched ringing with the room in disarray, that didn't stop him from returning to his weapon to wreak more havoc.

At some point, an order was given to leave the CP for another building. Bertoldo volunteered to stay behind to cover the withdrawal while he defended his position all night long through the bitter cold, with lack of sleep, and a hail of enemy fire.

That next morning, he moved his machine gun to another adjacent building which was another CP for a different battalion. From his new position, he'd broke up a heavy attack from an 88-mm gun along with 15 German troops trying to take the advance. By now, the Germans were probably getting sick and tired of dealing with this guy and took drastic measures to get rid of him. They moved an 88-mm weapon within a few feet of his new position so close that the barrel, which was about 16 feet long, was almost inside the building before firing into the room blasting him away once again.

I'm sure the German forces were pretty confident they had got him that time. They hadn't. Luckily, an American bazooka team, arrived and sent that heavy artillery to an early grave as a dazed Bertoldo went back to his machine gun to kill several enemy troops as they tried to withdraw.

As the enemy closed in, it was decided to withdraw from the second command post during the night but a German assault from tanks and heavy artillery disrupted their plan. Bertoldo, pulled off his signature move, and volunteered to stay at his post to protect his fellow soldiers to retreat. He served up a platter of white phosphorus grenades forcing the advancing troops to break up and retreat.

That was until a tank less than 50 yards away shot an explosive round into the building, destroying his weapon and blasting him across the room in a sick game of Déjà vu. The blast was so intense that it glued him to the wall before he was able to dislodge himself from the rubble, crawl over a dead comrade, and continue fighting with his rifle covering the withdrawal before the CP was finally abandoned.

Bertoldo, despite sustaining a concussion and internal injuries, managed to kill 40 German soldiers and wound many others in a restless 48-hour bitter battle that was so destructive that by the end of the fight in Hattan, 350 of the 365 houses had been destroyed. Bertoldo was promoted to Master Sergeant and would go on to receive the Medal of Honor for his efforts.

Interesting Facts

- Shortly after the war, Capt. Corson picked up a copy of *The Chicago Tribune* and saw on the front page a picture of President Truman pinning the Congressional Medal of Honor on the cook he sent off for guard duty.

- His son, David Valor Bertoldo, joined the Marine Corps during the Vietnam War and received the Bronze Star Medal.

- Bertoldo's grandson, David Christopher Bertoldo, served in the United States Army during the Gulf War.

THE AIR FORCE
WAS PART OF THE ARMY AIR CORPS IN WW2 AND DID NOT BECOME A SEPARATE BRANCH UNTIL 1947

ARTHUR O. BEYER

On January 15, 1945, Company C, 603rd Tank Destroyer Battalion found itself fighting two battles near Arloncourt in Belgium: a determined enemy line and an unforgiving winter.

Just shy of a month before, Germany had just begun the large campaign to split up the US and British forces to take back the port of Antwerp in what would kick off the Battle of the Bulge.

To accomplish the mission, a high priority target was to secure a transportation hub, Bastogne, Belgium. Seven main roads from the Ardennes forest converged at Bastogne. Controlling the roads would allow a further advancement through eastern Belgium to the port.

By December 22nd, US forces had found themselves encircled by German forces in the town of Bastogne, just 5 miles from Arloncourt. With the upper hand, the German commander sent a long-winded letter to the US commander to surrender or the German forces would "annihilate the U.S.A. troops in and near Bastogne." The US commander responded with an eight-word letter that read:

To the German Commander.

N U T S !

-The American Commander

130

The German forces interpreted the letter as basically saying, "Go to hell!" The Battle was on and the US were able to pierce through the encirclement with the help from elements of the US Third Army.

The 603rd, as part of the counterattack, continued to push hostile forces just north of Bastogne near Arloncourt but were held up by anti-tank machine guns, and small arms fire from German troops fighting from a maze of fox holes within a ridge.

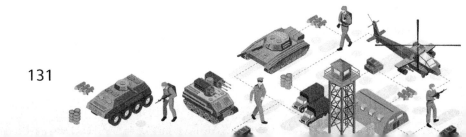

During the stand still, Corporal Arthur Beyer, armed with a 76 mm gun, noticed an enemy machine gun position, fired upon it killing one of the three-man crew. With the machine gun no longer being operated, he dismounted from the safety of his vehicle to cross an open and contested battle ground wielding nothing but his carbine and some grenades.

From the machine gun position, he captured the two remaining members as another machine gun position 250 yards away along the enemy's defensive line fired at him. Even with the concentrated heavy fire against him, he was able to encroach on the emplacement and threw a grenade into it killing one and capturing two more survivors.

Even though he wasn't ordered to, he continued on facing small arms fire and a bitter winter's day as he negotiated his way through a quarter mile of the enemy line along the ridge, attacking enemy troops in their foxholes with his gun and grenades.

By the end of his mission, he had killed 8 enemy forces, captured 18 prisoners, destroyed 2 machine gun emplacements, not to mention, not one, but two bazooka teams.

Because of his ballsy move to weaken the enemy line, he ensured his unit's advancement to push the German's back to the Siegfried Line, the opposing Maginot Line, and eventually take part in liberating the prisoners of the Buchenwald concentration camp. For his efforts, Arthur was awarded the Congressional Medal of Honor.

Interesting Fact

• Arloncourt is not too far from Luxembourg where Beyer's parents, Luxembourg immigrants, were from.

VERNON J. BAKER

During the year 1945, this next hero found himself fighting a battle on two different fronts.

Growing up, Baker, along with his two sisters, were orphaned after their parents were killed in a car accident. They were then raised by their grandparents in Cheyenne, Wyoming which is where a young man not wanting to follow his grandfather's footsteps into railroad work, decided to enlist in the Army to take a stand for his country which didn't take a stand for him based on the color of his skin.

The soon to be hero was Vernon Baker though the world may have never heard nor seen the man in action had he taken no for an answer.

The first time Baker went to talk with a recruiter, he walked into the local recruiting station only to be asked, "What do you want?" "I want to join the Army," Baker replied. The recruiter looked up at him from his large desk and said, "We don't have any quotas for you people." That could have been the end of this story, but as we will soon find out, Baker wasn't one to give up.

After three months of not being able to find a job, he swallowed his pride and went back to the recruiter station though this time he could feel adrenaline rushing in his veins as feelings swelled back up from his first attempt.

If the same guy was there and treated him the same, Baker was going to punch him in the nose. Luckily that wasn't the case. A nicer sergeant was there and asked him kindly as Baker walked in, "Can I help you?" Baker, with his hand still on the door answer, "Yes, I'd like to join the Army?" "Well come on in and sit down," the sergeant enthusiastically responded and got Baker squared away. He would soon find himself "voluntold" to Officer Candidate School (OCS) to fill a growing need for more black officers within the ranks.

During the time when the Army was still segregated, Lt Baker was assigned to the 270th Regiment, 92 Infantry Division, the same division as Lt John Fox, which was one of the first African American units to go into combat in WWII. On August 1, 1944, Baker landed in Naples, Italy and quickly proved himself as a valuable and skilled platoon leader studying past missions and training for weeks with his men in an extinct volcano crater just outside of Naples.

In April of 1945, Baker, as the only African American officer in his company, was ordered to lead his platoon within C Company on an assault against a German defense post... in a freakin' castle.

Aghinolfi, a medieval era castle, was a mere 40 miles west of Sommocolonia, stood atop a giant hill surrounded by a thick forest of trees. If there was ever a place to set up shop for war, this was it. It was an incredible vantage point for Germany and a menace to the US forces. It was a tower that stood over the battlefield and stood in the way of Allied forces ever pushing Germany out of Italy.

Baker would not be the first to lead an invasion of the castle. Three prior attempts to take it ended in utter disaster, and now it was Baker's turn.

At 0500 on April 5, 1945, Baker stepped off with 25 men, 70 percent which were replacements with little to zero combat experience, to siege that castle once and for all. Baker and his men charged ahead of the rest of the company and arrived 250 yards from the castle within two hours. Looking for a vantage point to set up a machine gun, Baker noticed two cylindrical objects sticking out of a slit in a mount at the edge of a hill.

Baker crawled up under the slit like a straight up ninja, stuck his M-1 in the hole and lit up two occupants with so much freedom it killed them. Nothing like a surprise attack early in the morning to kick off a day of battle.

Moving along, Lt Baker stumbled upon a well-camo'd machine gun nest and found the crew eating breakfast. What was Baker to do other than join them and offer a platter of bullets to compliment their Nazi feast. They must have been hungry because they ate so many bullets they died.

Afterwards, Capt. Runyon, Commander of Charlie Company, joined the group. who we will all grow to hate. Trust me, you will. Let's all hate him together, shall we?

After Capt. Runyon showed up, a German appeared from a draw in the ridge and hurled a grenade. That's really bad. Fortunately, the grenade hit the ground, bounced, and never exploded. That's really good. Baker shot the German as he tried to run and soon figured out that Runyon completely ghosted. What a maggot. But don't worry it gets worse. Baker, not having time to waste searching for their "fearless leader," grabbed a submachine from one of his squad leaders and proceeded into the draw alone.

From there he found a concealed entrance of a dugout which he blasted open with one of his four grenades. And then nothing happened. He was just about to peak his head in the hole to look when one German emerged from the entrance after the explosion which is exactly what no one in their right mind would do if someone blew open your door to your hideout. Oh well.

137

Baker shot him before throwing a housewarming grenade into the dugout killing three more. Moving his way closer he found another dugout and threw a third grenade followed by a spray from his machine gun taking out the two other Germans occupying that second dugout.

Leaving the draw and making his way back up the hill to his men, he found his men engaged with enemy forces who had found their location. Heavy mortar and machine gun fire from the castle saturated the area, killing and wounding several of Baker's men.

After several casualties and finally locating the mortar position behind a demolished house on an adjacent hill, Baker called in for artillery support which was initially denied. Why might you ask? Because his regiment did not believe that Baker had managed to get his barely trained group of men that close to the castle. Apparently, no other attempt had even gotten remotely as close in proximity as Baker had to the castle.

After a heated debate which I can only imagine involved very colorful language, the regiment finally fired and silenced the German mortars but only for so long.

By midafternoon, the Germans had launched a counterattack. As Baker directed his men for the oncoming assault, he searched with zero success to locate Capt. Runyon. Capt. Dirtbag ghosted again. Eventually, one of Baker's men informed him that Runyon was in a stone house at the edge of the battlefield.

Baker sprinted over to the house to found the company commander in the fetal position scared out of his mind. While the enemy was dropping bombs on the men he was

supposed to be leading, Runyon was busy trying not to drop some bombs in his trousers. As another barrage of mortars fell upon Baker's men, Runyon said to Baker, " Look, Baker, I'm going for reinforcements."

What he really meant to say was, " Look, Baker, I'm a coward and a maggot of a man. I'm not going back for reinforcements and you know I'm not going back for reinforcements. I'm actually going to run away to safety, but we both know that. Once I do get back to camp and when asked if reinforcements should be sent to save you and your men by my commanding officer, I'll tell them there is no reason to send reinforcements as those men 'were wasted'."

Baker, knowing full well no one was coming to save them, had to make a decision. After gathering up dog tags and enduring another mortar attack along with enemy fire from a platoon of German soldiers disguised as medics, he decided to withdraw.

His men wanted to stay but with 8 men out of the original 25 still alive and not to mention running low on ammo, he ordered the withdrawal while he himself picked up the rear to make sure his men could get back alive.

Baker killed another German trailing them before joining his men in retreat. Along the route back to camp, he lost two more men; one to a mortar round and another, the only medic, to an enemy sniper bringing the total down to six.

Before making it back to the battalion aid station, Baker discovered two additional machine-gun nests they had missed on the way up the mountain early that morning. Not putting his men at any more risk, he personally crawled over and destroyed each with grenades clearing the way for his men to safety.

After killing nine enemy dead soldiers, eliminating three machine gun positions, an observation post, and a dugout, you'd think he'd take the day off to recoup. Not this soldier. Not Baker. He volunteered to lead another battalion the next day through enemy mine fields back to the castle to find it deserted. This bloody victory helped paved the way for Allied forces to eventually push Germany out of Italy for good.

Interesting facts

- Baker decided not to wear his helmet and instead wore his dress uniform. If he was going to go out, he was going to go out looking sharp like the boss he was.

- He was one of seven African Americans to receive the Medal of Honor in WWII though he wouldn't receive it until 1997, almost 52 years after the battle at Castle Aghinolfi.

- He was the only living recipient at the time the Medal of Honor was awarded to the seven.

- He served in the Korean War as an Army parachutist and retired after serving over 25 years in the military.

- He would then work for the American Red Cross for almost 20 years.

- Baker wrote a book called *Lasting Valor* detailing the events of his life.

CONCLUSION

This brings us to the end of this book but not to the end of their stories, feats, and the legends they leave behind.

I hope that as you read about their lives and their time at war, about those who made it through and those who died on foreign soil, that you felt inspired and grateful for what they gave us.

Grateful that they fought.
Grateful that they changed the course of history.
Grateful for the lives we live as we stand on their giant shoulders.

As you turn on the final pages of this book, let's remember that we are also turning the final pages of a great generation that will soon no longer live among us.

They will become a piece of our history leaving behind a gift that has the potential of out living ourselves: their stories.

Until next time.

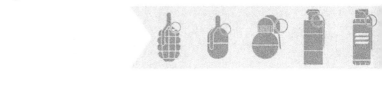

DID YOU ENJOY THE BOOK?

If you did, we are ecstatic. If not, please write your complaint to us and we will ensure we fix it.

If you're feeling generous, there is something important that you can help me with — tell other people that you enjoyed the book.

Please write about it on Amazon. These reviews will help more people find out about the book. It also lets Amazon know that we are providing high quality content for our readers. Even a few words and a star rating would go a long way.

If you have any stories that you think are interesting, please let us know. We would love to hear from you. Our email address is **chilimac@chilimacbook.com**

ABOUT
CHILI MAC BOOKS

Chili Mac Books is a small but fire crackin' publisher bringing hot stories of old back to life. Honing in on fascinating people, places, and events in history is their expertise with a mission to provide the tales of the extraordinary into the hands of curious minds around the world.

Whether highlighting legends of war, mavericks from around the world, or whacky stories you almost won't believe are true, Chili Mac Books lives to seek them out for the enjoyment of their loyal readers.

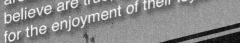

REFERENCES

27 Feb 1982, page 45 - Herald and review At Newspapers.com. (n.d.). Retrieved March 29, 2021, from https://www.newspapers.com/newspage/87666902/

AmericanlegionHQ. (2014, August 14). Medal of Honor Story: Hershel "WOODY" WILLIAMS. Retrieved March 29, 2021, from https://www.youtube.com/watch?v=lj-fZu7Y9DE

Arthur Beyer - recipient. (n.d.). Retrieved March 29, 2021, from https://valor.militarytimes.com/hero/205

Avcvideos. (2020, June 16). Iwo Jima Vet Harry Martin, a Usmc light Machine Gunner, tells his story (full interview). Retrieved March 29, 2021, from https://www.youtube.com/watch?v=lsM0hr10sWg

The battle of iwo jima. (n.d.). Retrieved March 29, 2021, from http://www.5thmarinedivision.com/the-battle-of-iwo-jima.html

Ben Salomon - recipient. (n.d.). Retrieved March 29, 2021, from https://valor.militarytimes.com/hero/237

The Ben Salomon's last stand took over 90 enemy soldiers with him. (2021, January 12). Retrieved March 29, 2021, from https://special-ops.org/medic-ben-salomons-last-stand-worth-medal-of-honor/

Bernard Bell - recipient. (n.d.). Retrieved March 29, 2021, from https://valor.militarytimes.com/hero/276

Braided in fire. (n.d.). Retrieved March 29, 2021, from https://braidedinfire.com/
Captain Ben Solomon. (n.d.). Retrieved March 29, 2021, from https://armyhistory.org/captain-ben-solomon/

Captured in HATTEN captain Corson's Speech Glenn Schmidt page 3: World War II ORAL HISTORY: World War 2 stories. (n.d.). Retrieved March 29, 2021, from http://www.tankbooks.com/stories/schmidt3.htm

Chan, A. (2019, September 30). Final spasm on SULFUR Island. Retrieved March 29, 2021, from https://www.historynet.com/final-spasm-on-sulfur-island.htm

Chapin, J. C. (n.d.). The Fifth Marine. Retrieved March 29, 2021, from https://www.usmcu.edu/Portals/218/Chapin_The%20Fifth%20Marine%20Division.pdf

Charles Coolidge - recipient. (n.d.). Retrieved March 29, 2021, from https://valor.militarytimes.com/hero/433
Chen, C. (n.d.). Battleship pennsylvania (bb-38). Retrieved March 29, 2021, from https://ww2db.com/ship_spec.php?ship_id=136
Doris Miller - recipient. (n.d.). Retrieved March 29, 2021, from https://valor.militarytimes.com/hero/20695

Charles Coolidge - recipient. (n.d.). Retrieved March 29, 2021, from https://valor.militarytimes.com/hero/433

Chen, C. (n.d.). Battleship pennsylvania (bb-38). Retrieved March 29, 2021, from https://ww2db.com/ship_spec.php?ship_id=136

Doris Miller - recipient. (n.d.). Retrieved March 29, 2021, from https://valor.militarytimes.com/hero/20695

Doris Miller. (2021, March 23). Retrieved March 29, 2021, from https://en.wikipedia.org/wiki/Doris_Miller

Doris' story. (n.d.). Retrieved March 29, 2021, from https://dorismillermemorial.org/doris-story/

Edwards, B. (n.d.). Jack Lucas: Youngest Man to Win the Congressional Medal of Honor. Retrieved March 29, 2021, from http://circanceast.beaufortccc.edu/BCCC/articles/December%202001/PDF/Story1.pdf

Edwards, J. (2016, June 25). Last seen alive with 8 bullets in a PISTOL, he was found DEAD, surrounded by 8 Dead Japanese and an Empty Pistol. Retrieved March 29, 2021, from https://www.warhistoryonline.com/featured/last-seen-alive-8-bullets-pistol-found-dead-surrounded-8-dead-japanese-empty-pistol.html

Edwin Hill - recipient. (n.d.). Retrieved March 29, 2021, from https://valor.militarytimes.com/hero/776

Edwin J. Hill. (n.d.). Retrieved March 29, 2021, from https://www.badassoftheweek.com/hill

Fox News. (2015, March 25). Remembering an American Hero: Col. ROBERT NETT. Retrieved March 29, 2021, from https://www.foxnews.com/story/remembering-an-american-hero-col-robert-nett

Frank Viviano, C. (2012, August 06). Almost-Forgotten heroes / Italian town honors black GIs who were shunned by their own country. Retrieved March 29, 2021, from https://www.sfgate.com/news/article/Almost-Forgotten-Heroes-Italian-town-honors-3240059.php

George Walters - recipient. (n.d.). Retrieved March 29, 2021, from https://valor.militarytimes.com/recipient.php?recipientid=84588

George Welch - recipient. (n.d.). Retrieved March 29, 2021, from https://valor.militarytimes.com/hero/22992

Gnam, C., & Wcmonahan@rushmore.com December 2. (2020, October 27). Operation Nordwind: The "other" Battle of the Bulge. Retrieved March 29, 2021, from https://warfarehistorynetwork.com/2018/12/22/operation-nordwind-the-other-battle-of-the-bulge/

Grave spotlight. (n.d.). Retrieved March 29, 2021, from http://www.cemeteryguide.com/gotw-gonzales.html

Harry Martin - recipient. (n.d.). Retrieved March 29, 2021, from https://valor.militarytimes.com/hero/1230

The hero of Signal mountain: The Army's last World War Ii Medal of Honor recipient. (n.d.). Retrieved March 29, 2021, from https://www.army.mil/article/237302/the_hero_of_signal_mountain_the_armys_last_world_war_ii_medal_of_honor_recipient

Hershel Williams - recipient. (n.d.). Retrieved March 29, 2021, from https://valor.militarytimes.com/hero/1354

History.com Editors. (2009, October 29). Battle of Guadalcanal. Retrieved March 29, 2021, from https://www.history.com/topics/world-war-ii/battle-of-guadalcanal

Indestructible. (n.d.). Retrieved March 29, 2021, from https://books.google.com/books?id=ZCj_AgAAQBAJ&pg=PA19&source=gbs_toc_r&cad=3#v=onepage&q&f=false

Jack Lucas. (2021, January 19). Retrieved March 29, 2021, from https://homeofheroes.com/heroes-stories/world-war-ii/jack-lucas/

Jacklyn Lucas - recipient. (n.d.). Retrieved March 29, 2021, from https://valor.militarytimes.com/hero/1427

Joedemadio. (2016, September 26). Thomas A. Baker – the battle for Saipan: Medal of Honor Monday. Retrieved March 29, 2021, from http://www.joedemadio.com/thomas-a-baker-the-battle-for-saipan-medal-of-honor-monday/

John Basilone - recipient. (n.d.). Retrieved March 29, 2021, from https://valor.militarytimes.com/hero/1829

John Basilone - recipient. (n.d.). Retrieved March 29, 2021, from https://valor.militarytimes.com/hero/1829

John Finn - recipient. (n.d.). Retrieved March 29, 2021, from https://valor.militarytimes.com/hero/2036

John Fox - recipient. (n.d.). Retrieved March 29, 2021, from https://valor.militarytimes.com/hero/2001

Kenneth Taylor - recipient. (n.d.). Retrieved March 29, 2021, from https://valor.militarytimes.com/hero/22980

Kingseed, C. C. (n.d.). The Saga of Vernon J. Baker. Retrieved March 29, 2021, from https://www.ausa.org/sites/default/files/Kingseed_0208.pdf

Kingseed, C. C. (n.d.). The Saga of Vernon J. Baker. Retrieved March 29, 2021, from https://www.ausa.org/sites/default/files/Kingseed_0208.pdf

LoProto, M., & *, N. (2019, June 04). The civilian Pearl Harbor hero. Retrieved March 29, 2021, from https://visitpearlharbor.org/the-civilian-pearl-harbor-hero/

LT John William Finn. (n.d.). Retrieved March 29, 2021, from https://militaryhallofhonor.com/honoree-record.php?id=21

Malloryk. (2020, February 16). The incredible story of jack Lucas: The Youngest Medal of Honor recipient in World War II: The National WWII Museum: New Orleans. Retrieved March 29, 2021, from https://www.nationalww2museum.org/war/articles/incredible-story-jack-lucas-youngest-medal-honor-recipient-world-war-ii

Malloryk. (2020, September 24). Medal of Honor RECIPIENT VERNON baker: "set THE example": The National WWII Museum: New Orleans. Retrieved March 29, 2021, from https://www.nationalww2museum.org/war/articles/medal-of-honor-recipient-vernon-baker

The man who wouldn't GIVE up-Samuel G. Fuqua untold story(official TRAILER). (2020, March 04). Retrieved March 29, 2021, from https://www.youtube.com/watch?v=-yFTbV2Leuo

A Marine named Mitch : An Autobiography of MITCHELL Paige, Colonel, U.S. Marine Corps Retired : Paige, Mitchell. (1975, January 01). Retrieved March 29, 2021, from https://archive.org/details/marinenamedmitch00mitc/page/n1/mode/2up

Medal of Honor MONDAY: Marine Corps Cpl. Hershel Williams. (n.d.). Retrieved March 29, 2021, from https://www.defense.gov/Explore/Features/story/Article/1772607/medal-of-honor-monday-marine-corps-cpl-hershel-williams/

MedalOfHonorBook. (2011, September 27). Charles Coolidge, Medal of Honor, WWII. Retrieved March 29, 2021, from https://www.youtube.com/watch?v=hDq4PxzxWUw

MedalOfHonorBook. (2011, September 27). Mitchell Paige, Medal of Honor, WWII. Retrieved March 29, 2021, from https://www.youtube.com/watch?v=FA3jz6H3H0k

MedalOfHonorBook. (2011, September 27). Van Barfoot, Medal of Honor, WWII. Retrieved March 29, 2021, from https://www.youtube.com/watch?v=yUVF8jkzTF8

Melissa. (2017, January 11). The amazing heroism of Ben I. SALOMON- the Army dentist who KILLED 98 attacking enemy SOLDIERS SINGLE-HANDEDLY. Retrieved March 29, 2021, from http://www.todayifoundout.com/index.php/2017/01/amazing-heroism-ben-l-salomon-army-dentist-killed-98-attacking-enemy-soldiers-single-handedly/

Mendes, C. (2019, July 25). Mitchell Paige: The man who took on 2,500 Japanese Soldiers & Won. Retrieved March 29, 2021, from https://www.warhistoryonline.com/instant-articles/mitchell-paige-took-japanese.html

Mitchell Paige - recipient. (n.d.). Retrieved March 29, 2021, from https://valor.militarytimes.com/hero/2410

Nationalmuseum.af.mil. (n.d.). Retrieved March 29, 2021.

Nedforney.com. (n.d.). Retrieved March 29, 2021, from https://nedforney.com/index.php/2019/06/13/peter-tomich-usn-medal-of-honor-pearl-harbor/

Nedforney.com. (n.d.). Retrieved March 29, 2021, from https://nedforney.com/index.php/2019/06/13/peter-tomich-usn-medal-of-honor-pearl-harbor/

Network, W. (2019, November 29). Meet "Manila JOHN" Basilone: A World War II MARINE HERO. Retrieved March 29, 2021, from https://nationalinterest.org/blog/buzz/meet-%E2%80%9Cmanila-john%E2%80%9D-basilone-world-war-ii-marine-hero-100302

Network, W. (2019, November 29). Meet "Manila JOHN" Basilone: A World War II MARINE HERO. Retrieved March 29, 2021, from https://nationalinterest.org/blog/buzz/meet-%E2%80%9Cmanila-john%E2%80%9D-basilone-world-war-ii-marine-hero-100302?page=0%2C1

Nye, L. (2020, October 22). This Army dentist DIED mowing down 98 attacking Japanese soldiers. Retrieved March 29, 2021, from https://www.wearethemighty.com/mighty-history/army-dentist-medal-of-honor/

Oregonian/OregonLive, M. (2012, January 14). Ship repair equipment, including crane that may have played heroic role at Pearl Harbor, is for sale. Retrieved March 29, 2021, from https://www.oregonlive.com/oregonatwar/2012/01/going_going_gone_ship_repair_e.html

Patterson, M. (n.d.). Samuel Glenn Fuqua, Rear ADMIRAL, United States Navy. Retrieved March 29, 2021, from http://www.arlingtoncemetery.net/sgfuqua.html

Pearl harbor Hero Stories: George Welch & KENNETH TAYLOR. (2020, December 16). Retrieved March 29, 2021, from https://www.warbirds-eaa.org/pearl-harbor-hero-stories-george-welch-kenneth-taylor/

Pearl Harbor: Why, How, Fleet salvage and Final Appraisal. (n.d.). Retrieved March 29, 2021, from https://www.history.navy.mil/research/library/online-reading-room/title-list-alphabetically/p/pearl-harbor-why-how.html

Pennsylvania III (BATTLESHIP No. 38). (n.d.). Retrieved March 29, 2021, from https://www.history.navy.mil/research/histories/ship-histories/danfs/p/pennsylvania-ii.html

Peter Tomich - recipient. (n.d.). Retrieved March 29, 2021, from https://valor.militarytimes.com/hero/2576

PFC David M. Gonzales. (n.d.). Retrieved March 29, 2021, from https://militaryhallofhonor.com/honoree-record.php?id=1410

Philip Rasmussen - recipient. (n.d.). Retrieved March 29, 2021, from https://valor.militarytimes.com/hero/49417

Profile.php?id=678073688. (n.d.). The few who got up. Retrieved March 29, 2021, from https://www.defensemedianetwork.com/stories/the-few-who-got-up/

Published by the Church of Scientology International. (n.d.). Retrieved March 29, 2021, from https://www.freedommag.org/english/vol31i2/page33.htm

Remarks on presenting the Congressional Medal of Honor posthumously to CAPTAIN Ben I. Salomon and CAPTAIN Jon E. Swanson. (2002, May 01). Retrieved March 29, 2021, from https://www.presidency.ucsb.edu/documents/remarks-presenting-the-congressional-medal-honor-posthumously-captain-ben-l-salomon-and

Remembering Colonel Mitchell Paige. (n.d.). Retrieved March 29, 2021, from https://eldredpawwiimuseum.com/remembering-colonel-mitchell-paige/

Remembering rear Admiral Samuel G. Fuqua and Pearl Harbor. (2020, December 07). Retrieved March 29, 2021, from https://www.forkunion.com/news/remembering-rear-admiral-samuel-g-fuqua-and-pearl-harbor#gref

Robert Hodges, J. (2018, February 16). How the 'Buffalo Soldiers' helped turn the tide in Italy during World War II. Retrieved March 29, 2021, from https://www.militarytimes.com/military-honor/black-military-history/2018/02/14/how-the-buffalo-soldiers-helped-turn-the-tide-in-italy-during-world-war-ii/

Robert nett - recipient. (n.d.). Retrieved March 29, 2021, from https://valor.militarytimes.com/hero/2727

Samuel Fuqua - recipient. (n.d.). Retrieved March 29, 2021, from https://valor.militarytimes.com/hero/2853

Says:, J., Says:, L., Says:, M., Says:, M., & Says:, A. (2017, January 11). Van T. BARFOOT. Retrieved March 29, 2021, from http://www.nww2m.com/2012/03/van-t-barfoot/

Sclischede. (2010, September 26). USS Arizona explosion and fire. Retrieved March 29, 2021, from https://www.youtube.com/watch?v=ujquq7IU0uY

Simkins, J. (2019, February 19). Valor Friday: The Legend of John Basilone. Retrieved March 29, 2021, from https://www.marinecorpstimes.com/news/your-army/2018/06/29/valor-friday-the-legend-of-john-basilone/

Simkins, J. (2020, February 20). 'If fear takes over, you BECOME Useless' - Medal of Honor recipient recounts the Battle of Iwo Jima. Retrieved March 29, 2021, from https://www.militarytimes.com/off-duty/military-culture/2020/02/19/if-fear-takes-over-you-become-useless-medal-of-honor-recipient-recounts-the-battle-of-iwo-jima/

Tara. (2019, May 01). This day in History: Lt. COL. Phillip Rasmussen, hero of Pearl Harbor. Retrieved March 29, 2021, from https://www.taraross.com/post/tdih-pajama-pilot

Tara. (2020, June 28). This day in History: Thomas A. Baker's bravery during A banzai charge. Retrieved March 29, 2021, from https://www.taraross.com/post/tdih-thomas-baker-moh

Tara. (2020, September 28). This day in History: Van T. Barfoot versus three German tanks. Retrieved March 29, 2021, from https://www.taraross.com/post/tdih-van-barfoot-moh

Thomas Baker - recipient. (n.d.). Retrieved March 29, 2021, from https://valor.militarytimes.com/hero/2987

Thomas W. Cutrer and T. Michael Parrish, W. (2020, January 20). How Dorie miller's BRAVERY helped fight navy racism. Retrieved March 29, 2021, from https://www.navytimes.com/military-honor/salute-veterans/2019/11/01/how-dorie-millers-bravery-helped-fight-bigotry-in-the-navy/

Tomich. (n.d.). Retrieved March 29, 2021, from http://gonebutnotforgotten.homestead.com/Tomich.html

Trofimuk, A. (2019, June 07). STORIES of HONOR: Vito Bertoldo's heroic actions in wwii earned Congressional Medal of Honor. Retrieved March 29, 2021, from https://herald-review.com/news/local/stories-of-honor-vito-bertoldos-heroic-actions-in-wwii-earned-congressional-medal-of-honor/article_bd03c4fd-40b1-548c-b7d0-4a6ba1df1232.html

U.S.S. Arizona Facts. (n.d.). Retrieved March 29, 2021, from http://ussarizonafacts.org/fuqua.htm

USS Pennsylvania (BB-38) ACTION REPORT: 7 Dec 1941. (n.d.). Retrieved March 29, 2021, from https://www.ibiblio.org/hyperwar/USN/ships/logs/BB/bb38-Pearl.html

USS Utah hero: PETER TOMICH. (n.d.). Retrieved March 29, 2021, from https://www.ussutah1941.org/peter-tomich-moh.html

Van Barfoot - recipient. (n.d.). Retrieved March 29, 2021, from https://valor.militarytimes.com/hero/3065

Vernon Baker - recipient. (n.d.). Retrieved March 29, 2021, from https://valor.militarytimes.com/hero/3067

Vito Bertoldo - recipient. (n.d.). Retrieved March 29, 2021, from https://valor.militarytimes.com/hero/3071

The warrior of kāneʻohe: Pearl harbor's first medal of honor recipient: The sextant. (2019, December 09). Retrieved March 29, 2021, from https://usnhistory.navylive.dodlive.mil/2016/12/06/the-warrior-of-kaneohe-pearl-harbors-first-medal-of-honor-recipient/

WEST VIRGINIANS awarded the Medal of honor. (n.d.). Retrieved March 29, 2021, from http://www.wvculture.org/history/wvmemory/stutlmoh.html

Who broke the sound barrier first? (n.d.). Retrieved March 29, 2021, from https://www.456fis.org/GEORGE_WELCH_SOUND_BARRIER.htm

WW2 medal of Honor Recipient Hershel "WOODY" Williams I Memoirs OF WWII #7. (2018, November 02). Retrieved March 29, 2021, from https://www.youtube.com/watch?v=O9TqQWLtBJk

Youngest marine to get medal of honor. (2008, June 06). Retrieved March 29, 2021, from https://www.latimes.com/archives/la-xpm-2008-jun-06-me-lucas6-story.html